"*Charts on the Book of Revelation* is a useful supplement ‗ oth the church and the academy. Wilson's charts cover a range of h⸏ ₌ issues that will guide the careful student in making more viable int ₌ ook. An excellent resource to use with today's visual learners as the₌ ‗y."

—ROBERT WALTER WALL
The Paul T. Walls Professor of Biblical and Wesleyan Studies
Chair, Department of Christian Scriptures
Seattle Pacific University
Author of *Revelation* in the New International Biblical Commentary series

"This is an enormously helpful book, bringing together in visual form extensive comparative data both from and about Revelation. Not to be confused with prophecy charts of a bygone era, here we find charts on everything from various views of authorship and date to extensive lists of scriptural allusions and verbal parallels, from John's use of symbols and numbers to all references to angels and demons—and much else—seventy-nine in all. Each is carefully annotated with the source of the information. While the parallels are not always convincing, they always provide an interesting place to start and will save the reader much time in collecting data."

—DAVID L. BARR
Brage Golding Distinguished Professor
Wright State University
Editor of *Reading the Book of Revelation*

"Wilson's *Charts on the Book of Revelation* synthesizes an enormous amount of material relevant to the study of the Revelation of John and makes it available in a clear, useful, and unusual format for students of the Bible."

—DAVID E. AUNE
Professor of New Testament
University of Notre Dame
Author of the three-volume *Revelation* in the Word Biblical Commentary series

"If you are looking for helpful maps and charts that are substantive and revealing in regard to the book of Revelation, look no further than Mark Wilson's excellent resource. I know of no better collection of materials that illuminates Revelation than this resource."

—BEN WITHERINGTON III
Professor of New Testament Interpretation
Asbury Theological Seminary
Author of *Revelation* in the New Cambridge Bible Commentary series

"*Charts on the Book of Revelation* is a useful tool for teachers and a helpful guide for students to many complex and disputed issues related to the interpretation of that biblical book. The charts provide handy thumbnail sketches and collections of data on the contents of the book itself, its connections with other biblical and extracanonical works, its historical setting, and various 'brands' of its reception-history. Teachers and students from a great variety of cultural and theological backgrounds will all find that this book enhances their access to and communication of the book of Revelation."

—ADELA YARBRO COLLINS
Buckingham Professor of New Testament Criticism and Interpretation
Yale Divinity School
Author of *The Apocalypse* and *Crisis & Catharsis: The Power of the Apocalypse*

"More than any book in the Bible, Revelation needs to be visualized to be understood. *Charts on the Book of Revelation* is a major step forward in doing just that. Every pastor and Bible teacher will benefit from using these charts in their study and as overheads when teaching and preaching through the book."

—**GRANT R. OSBORNE**
Professor of New Testament
Trinity Evangelical Divinity School
Author of *Revelation* in the Baker Exegetical Commentary on the New Testament series

"This is a novel idea and an inspired one. These charts will be invaluable to anyone studying the book of Revelation in detail."

—**RICHARD BAUCKHAM**
Professor of New Testament Studies and Bishop Wardlaw Professor
University of St. Andrews
Author of *The Theology of the Book of Revelation*

Charts on the
Book of Revelation

Literary, Historical,
and Theological
Perspectives

Charts on the Book of Revelation

Literary, Historical, and Theological Perspectives

Mark Wilson

Kregel
Academic & Professional

Charts on the Book of Revelation: Literary, Historical, and Theological Perspectives

© 2007 by Mark Wilson
Maps © Tim Dowley, Three's Company. Used by permission.

Published by Kregel Publications, a division of Kregel, Inc., P.O. Box 2607, Grand Rapids, MI 49501.

ISBN 978-0-8254-3939-1

Printed in the United States of America

07 08 09 10 11 / 5 4 3 2

Contents

Preface

While working on this volume, I mentioned to friends and colleagues that I was preparing a book of charts on Revelation. Invariably I detected an unspoken reaction like, "Just what we need, another book of charts on Revelation." This volume, however, should prove different from other charts books that have appeared. For years commentators have developed charts to illustrate their reading of Revelation, which was usually from a dispensational and futurist perspective. From my earliest days as a Christian, some thirty-two years ago, I recall seeing large wall charts that displayed the chronology of last-days events supposedly depicted in Revelation and Daniel.

In the latter part of the twentieth century, new methods of reading the text have opened fresh perspectives for examining Revelation. Literary readings particularly have examined the complex intertextuality and intratextuality of the book. From my perspective, Revelation is one of the most extraordinary documents ever written, with new levels awaiting discovery on each reading. For these reasons, of all the books of the Bible, Revelation lends itself best to visualization in charts.

The format used in most contemporary commentaries, though, lends little room for charts. For example, Osborne in his 869-page commentary has only three charts (pp. 233, 340, 757), and the first is related to the Gospels rather than Revelation. Beale offers eight charts in the introduction (pp. 70–71, 73–75, 90–91, 106, 107, 119, 128, 134–35), but only four (pp. 809–10, 874, 992, 1005) in the rest of his 1,245-page commentary. For a new generation of students who are primarily visual learners, charts are an important pedagogical tool. Information that might take pages of text to explain can be distilled into an easily comprehensible chart. Other books of charts with limited material on Revelation include H. Wayne House and Randall Price's *Charts of Bible Prophecy* (Grand Rapids: Zondervan, 2003), H. Wayne House's *Chronological and Background Charts of the New Testament* (Grand Rapids: Zondervan, 1981), and *Nelson's Complete Book of Bible Maps and Charts* (Nashville: Thomas Nelson, 1993).

Many of the charts in this volume were initially developed during my doctoral research, and some were first published in my doctoral thesis accepted at the University of South Africa in 1996. Other charts were prepared by me for various writing projects or for presentation in church or seminary lectures. One distinctive of these charts is that the material in Revelation is primary and thus usually listed first, with Old Testament and extrabiblical literature secondary. This arrangement helps to underscore the hermeneutical principle that any context must be interpreted through the primary text of Revelation. Breaking the verses down into sections of a, b, c, etc., has been avoided within the charts as much as possible. Usually the applicable portion of the verse in question is evident. For chart 32, however, "Structure of the Seven Letters in Revelation 2–3," more detailed verse breakdowns were unavoidable. Notes related to each chart, with abbreviated bibliographic references, appear after the charts. A full bibliography concludes the book.

I thank my wife, Dindy, for her patient editorial work in verifying many of the references in the volume. I also thank Jim Weaver and Dennis Hillman of Kregel Publications for their patience with the manuscript, which was delivered long past its promised date. Tim Dowley did an excellent job in preparing the maps from the material that I supplied. I especially want to dedicate this volume to my former students at Oral Roberts University, Regent University, and Fuller Seminary Northwest, who have studied Revelation with me and have given me valuable feedback on the charts.

Abbreviations

Ancient and Extrabiblical Sources

1 Clem.	*1 Clement* (The Apostolic Fathers)
1 En.	*1 Enoch* (OT Pseudepigrapha)
2 Macc.	2 Maccabees (OT Apocrypha)
3 Macc.	3 Maccabees (OT Apocrypha)
5QNJ	Dead Sea Scroll (5Q New Jerusalem)
Adv. Haer.	Irenaeus, *Adversus Haereses* (*Against Heresies*)
Adv. Marc.	Tertullian, *Adversus Marcion* (*Against Marcion*)
Ann.	Tacitus, *Annals*
Ant.	Josephus, *Antiquities of the Jews*
Bar.	Baruch (OT Apocrypha)
Carm. Saec.	Horace, *Carmen Saeculare*
Dial.	Justin, *Dialogue with Trypho*
Dom.	Suetonius, *Domitian*
Ep.	Augustine, *Epistles*
Epig.	Martial, *Epigrams*
Gen. litt.	Augustine, *De Genesi ad Litteram*
Hist.	Tacitus, *Historiae*
Hist. eccl.	Eusebius, *Historia Ecclesiastica* (*Ecclesiastical History*)
IGR	*Inscriptiones Graecae ad Res Romanas Pertinentes*
J.W.	Josephus, *Jewish War*
Nat.	Pliny, *Natural History*
Nero	Suetonius, *Nero*
OCD	*Oxford Classical Dictionary,* 3rd ed. (1996)
OGIS	*Orientis Graeci Inscriptiones Selectae*
Or.	Dio Chrysostom, *Orations*
Pss. Sol.	*Psalms of Solomon* (OT Pseudepigrapha)
Sat.	Juvenal, *Satires*
SIG³	W. Dittenberger, *Sylloge Inscriptionum Graecarum,* 3rd ed. (1915–1924)
Silv.	Statius, *Silvae*
Sir.	Sirach/Ecclesiasticus (OT Apocrypha)
Tob.	Tobit (OT Apocrypha)
Trist.	Ovid, *Tristia*
Wis.	Wisdom of Solomon (OT Apocrypha)

Bible Versions and Translations

KJV	King James Version
LXX	Septuagint
MT	Masoretic Text
NIV	New International Version
NKJV	New King James Version
NLT	New Living Translation
NRSV	New Revised Standard Version
NT	New Testament
OT	Old Testament

REB	Revised English Bible
UBS³	*The Greek New Testament*, 3rd ed. United Bible Societies
UBS⁴	*The Greek New Testament*, 4th ed. United Bible Societies

1. Authorship of Revelation

John the Apostle	
Pro	**Con**
Patristic testimony: Justin, Papias, Melito, Irenaeus, Origen, Tertullian, and Hippolytus affirm apostolic authorship of Rev.	Marcion, Dionysius, and Alogoi testify against apostolic authorship
Apocryphal *Acts of John* (88–90) portrays apostle as ministering among seven churches	Papias (*Hist. eccl.* 3.39.4–6) speaks of two Johns whose tombs are in Ephesus
Gnostic *Apocryphon of John* identifies Apocalyptist as brother of James and son of Zebedee	Lack of apostolic claim: absence of explicit identification as son of Zebedee, beloved disciple, or elder
Muratorian Canon (late 2nd c.) identifies author of Rev. with author of fourth gospel	Stylistic differences: grammatical solecisms in Greek text contrast with accurate and clear text of fourth gospel
Apocalypse and fourth gospel share some common ideas, theology, and terminology	Theological differences—theology, Christology, and eschatology—are too distinct between Rev., fourth gospel, and 1 John
Like the other apostles Paul (Rom. 1:1; Titus 1:1), James (James 1:1), and Peter (2 Peter 1:1), Apocalyptist calls himself a servant in the book's introduction (1:1; cf. 22:9)	Apocalyptist regards himself as a prophet, calling his work a prophecy six times (1:3; 19:10; 22:7, 10, 18, 19)
Ephesian church tested so-called apostles (2:2) and found them false, so must have judged John to be a true apostle	Twelve apostles spoken of as past figures in 21:14, so unlikely that Apocalyptist was the son of Zebedee
Epistolary greeting "Grace and peace" (1:4) is apostolic and opens all Pauline letters as well as 1 & 2 Peter	Aged apostle would be too old to produce virile imaginativeness of the Apocalypse
Epistolary closing "The grace" in 22:21 is apostolic and closes every Pauline letter	
Rev. to be read publicly (1:3), which is similar to Paul's injunction to have his letters read publicly (1 Thess. 5:27; Col. 4:16; 1 Tim. 4:13) and suggests apostolic authority and inspiration	

John the Elder	
Pro	**Con**
Papias (*Hist. eccl.* 3.39.4–5) speaks of two Johns: a disciple and an elder	Eusebius misunderstood Papias's distinction between the elder and apostle
Dionysius (cf. *Hist. eccl.* 3.39.6) states there were two Johns and two tombs in Ephesus, both tombs called John's	Dionysius's comment based on a traveler's report, and his suggestion is only tentative
Papias (*Hist. eccl.* 3.39.6–7) says he actually heard the elder John, so Eusebius says it is probable that it was this John who "saw" Rev.	Inconclusive that John the elder ever existed
John the elder known to Ephesian community through his letters	Early church mistaken in belief that apostle lived in Ephesus because presence of two Johns would have caused confusion

2. Date of Revelation

Evidence	Early Date (ca. A.D. 69)	Late Date (ca. A.D. 95)
Christian literary evidence	Domitian ruled eleven months in Rome until his father Vespasian returned from the Jewish War; perhaps Irenaeus, wrong on other dates, got the evidence confused	Firm tradition in Irenaeus (*Adv. Haer.* 5.30.3): "Seen not long ago, but almost in our own day, at the close of the principate [reign] of Domitian"
Church situation	Galatians quickly deserted (Gal. 1:6) and Paul's companions shipwrecked in their faith (1 Tim. 1:19), so period needed for decline can be brief	Decline takes time: Ephesus has lost first love; Sardis is dead and Laodicea is now lukewarm; rise of Nicolaitan party shows time lapse
Historical situation	60s a turbulent time in Roman Empire with Nero's suicide and year of four emperors	Reign of terror begins against Domitian's enemies in A.D. 93
Persecution by Domitian	No literary evidence exists for Domitian persecuting Christians; he killed only presumed political opponents	Eusebius (*Hist. eccl.* 3.17–20) calls Domitian a second Nero, who persecuted and martyred Christians
Food sacrificed to idols (2:14, 20)	Problematic "hot" issue among several churches in Asia	Issue appears resolved with only brief mention in *Didache* (6.3) and not mentioned by Ignatius
Asian earthquake in A.D. 60 (cf. 3:17)	Laodicea refused aid from Rome because of civic independence; her wealth enables city to begin rebuilding right away	Devastation of earthquake at Laodicea required decades to restore city to former grandeur
Great Tribulation (7:9–14)	Fiercest persecution of Christians occurred under Nero after Rome's fire of 64; Tacitus (*Ann.* 15.44) and Clement (*1 Clem.* 6:1) speak of "great multitudes" of Christians dying	Asian persecution limited only to Antipas in Pergamum; expectation of greater persecution suggests later period
Temple in Jerusalem (11:1–2)	That the temple can be measured suggests it is still standing	Reference to temple is from an earlier source incorporated into the vision
Political situation (13:1–8)	Beast need not refer to Domitian but could refer to earlier Caesar (Nero)	Beast depicts Caesar's (Domitian's) successful war against saints and his worship by all earth dwellers
Nero *redivivus* (resurrection) myth (13:3, 12, 14; 17:8)	First Nero pretender appears on Aegean island of Cythnus in 69 and his body is displayed publicly in Ephesus; myth circulates soon after	References to resurrected Beast suggest time period needed for myth to arise following Nero's death in 68
Roman imperial cult (13:11–15)	Cult active in Asia since Augustus authorized temple in Pergamum in 29 B.C., and Tiberius authorized temple in Smyrna in A.D. 26	Worship of emperor as "Lord and God" reached zenith under Domitian; temple to Flavian dynasty built in Ephesus in A.D. 89/90
666 (13:18)	Gematria (numerology) in Hebrew fits only Nero	Apocalyptic tradition is now historicized and fulfilled in Flavian dynasty
Name "Babylon" (14:8; 16:19; 17:5; 18:2, 10, 21)	If 1 Peter (5:13) and Rev. are dated before A.D. 70, this is early literary evidence for use of "Babylon"	Use of "Babylon" not documented in literary sources until after A.D. 70
Seven emperors (17:9–11)	Nero is the fifth "fallen" emperor of the principate	Domitian is the fifth "fallen" emperor among the principate's tyrants

3. Roman Empire in the Late First Century A.D.

		Roman Empire in the 60s			Roman Empire under Domitian (88–96)
64	July 19	Fire in Rome	88		False Nero appears in Asia and finds refuge among Parthians
65	April	Pisonian conspiracy to kill Nero foiled	89	Jan. 1	Saturninus, governor of Upper Germany, revolts
	Spring?	Persecution of the church begins		Spring	Revolt of Chatti in Germany
	Summer?	Martyrdom of Peter in Rome		Summer	Revolt of Dacians on the Danube; First Pannonian War
		30,000 die of plague in Rome; hurricane at Campagna	91		Governor of Asia, G. Vettulenus Civica Cerealis, assassinated by Domitian
		Former governor of Asia, L. Antistius Vetus, condemned by Nero			Manius Acilius Glabrio exiled for atheism
66	June	Vinician conspiracy to kill Nero foiled		Fall	Grain famine causes Domitian in the spring to issue edict to destroy vineyards
	July	Jews capture Masada and halt temple sacrifice for the emperor	92	May	Sarmatians and Suebi revolt on the Danube; second Pannonian War
	Aug.–?	Gentiles massacre tens of thousands of Jews in Caesarea and Alexandria			Famine in Pisidian Antioch
	Sept. 25	Nero begins performance tour in Greece	93	Fall	Domitian's reign of terror begins
	Oct.– Nov.	Cestius attacks Jerusalem but forced to retreat in defeat			Apollonius of Tyana travels to Rome, where he is arrested
		Former governor of Asia, M. Barea Soranus, condemned by Nero	94		Domitian's reign of terror continues
66 or 67?		Martyrdom of Paul in Rome	95	May	Flavius Clemens (first cousin of Domitian) killed
67	July	Jewish forces defeated at Jotopata; Josephus captured			His wife Flavia Domitilla (niece of Domitian) banished to Pontia (Eusebius) or Pandateria (Cassius Dio [this form used by *OCD*])
68		Nero returns from Greece		Summer	Third Pannonian War?
	March	Vindex revolts at Lugdunum, Gaul			Apollonius escapes condemnation and returns to Asia
	April 3	Galba proclaimed emperor at Carthago Nova, Spain	96	Sept. 18	Domitian murdered by his attendant Stephanus
	May	Vindex defeated at Vesontio by German legions			
	June 8	Galba recognized by Senate			
	June 9	Nero commits suicide by sword			
	June 20	Vespasian and Trajan occupy Jericho; Jerusalem surrounded			
	October	Galba arrives in Rome from Tarraco, Spain			
	Fall	False Nero executed on Aegean island of Cythnus; corpse shipped from Ephesus to Rome			
		Famine in Rome			

69	Jan. 2	Vitellius acclaimed emperor by Rhine legions at Colonia Agrippina			
	Jan. 10	Galba adopts Piso as heir to principate			
	Jan. 15	Otho usurps principate, assassinating Galba and Piso			
	Feb.	Titus visits Ephesus to conspire with Governor C. Fonteius Agrippa			
	March	Otho leaves Rome to fight Vitellius			
	April 14–16	Otho's army defeated at first battle of Cremona; he commits suicide			
	May	Vitellius recognized by Senate			
	Late June	Capitol burned by foreign mercenaries when Vitellius arrives in Rome			
	July 1, 3	Vespasian proclaimed emperor in Alexandria and Judea			
	Aug.	Batavian revolt along the Rhine under Civilis			
	Sept.	Dacian revolt along the Danube			
	Oct. 18	Moon turned to blood in lunar eclipse			
	Oct. 24–25	Flavians under Antonius Primus defeat Vitellians at Cremona with the city subsequently burned			
	Dec. 18	Capitol burned, including temple of Jupiter Optimus Maximus			
	Dec. 20	Rome captured by Flavian army under Antonius Primus; Vitellius killed in the Forum			
	Dec.	Domitian with Mucianus begin to govern jointly in his father's absence from Rome			
		Flood of Tiber in Rome			
70	Jan.	Gauls revolt			
	Winter	1st, 4th, 16th, & 22nd legions mutiny in Germany			
	May 1	Titus besieges Jerusalem			
	June	Domitian and Mucianus leave Rome to campaign in Gaul			
	Sept. 26	Titus captures Jerusalem and destroys the temple			
	Oct.	Vespasian arrives in Rome to assume principate			

4. Time Line of the First-Century Church in Asia

A.D. 30	Acts 2:9	Jews from Asia at Pentecost in Jerusalem
49	Acts 16:6	Paul on his second missionary journey forbidden by Holy Spirit from preaching in Asia
49	Acts 16:8–11	Paul has vision of Macedonian man in Troas
52	Acts 18:19–22	Paul visits synagogue in Ephesus on way to Jerusalem
52	Acts 18:19	Priscilla and Aquila remain in Ephesus
53	Acts 18:24–27	Apollos speaks in Ephesus synagogue, is instructed by Priscilla and Aquila, and leaves for Corinth
53–55	Acts 19:1–41	Paul ministers in Ephesus for over 2 years
53	Acts 19:8–9	Paul speaks in synagogue for 3 months
53–54	Acts 19:9–10	Paul lectures daily in hall of Tyrannus for 2 years, and Jews and Greeks of Asia hear the word
55	1 Cor. 16:19	Paul writes 1 Corinthians from Ephesus, sending greetings from the churches of Asia
55	2 Cor. 2:1; 12:14; 13:1–2	Paul makes "painful" second visit to Corinth from Ephesus
55	Acts 19:22; 1 Cor. 4:17; 16:10	Timothy and Erastus are sent first to Macedonia, then Corinth
55	1 Cor. 16:11; 2 Cor. 10:1–11	Timothy apparently returns to Ephesus with news that Paul is under personal attack
55	1 Cor. 15:31–32; 2 Cor. 1:3–11	Paul fights "wild beasts" in Ephesus, experiencing great suffering, pressure, and hardships in Asia
55	Acts 20:1; cf. 2 Cor. 1:1	Paul leaves Ephesus, probably with Timothy, after the riot in theater
55	2 Cor. 2:12–13	Paul searches for Titus in Troas, leaving behind "open door" there for Macedonia
55	1 Cor. 16:19; Rom. 16:3	Aquila and Priscilla depart Ephesus for Rome
56	Acts 20:5	Paul's seven companions, including Trophimus of Asia, sail to Troas, carrying collection for Jerusalem church
56	Acts 20:6–12	Paul and Luke arrive in Troas; Paul raises Eutychus from the dead
56	Acts 20:13–15; 21:1	Paul walks to Assos, then sails with eight companions to Asian islands of Lesbos (Mitylene), Chios, Samos, and Cos on way to Jerusalem
56	Acts 20:17–38	Paul meets Ephesian elders in Miletus
56	Acts 21:27–29; 24:18–19	Jews from Asia charge Paul with bringing Trophimus, an Ephesian Gentile believer, into the temple area
59	Acts 27:2–5	Paul sails on Adramyttium-based ship to Myra
59	Acts 27:7	Paul sails off Cnidus on voyage to Rome
61–62	Eph. 1:1; Col. 1:2; 4:13, 15–16	From Rome, Paul writes Asian churches at Ephesus, Colossae, Laodicea, and Hierapolis
61–62	Philem. 1–2	From Rome, Paul writes Philemon, Apphia, and Archippus at Colossae
63	1 Peter 1:1; 5:13	From Rome (Babylon), Peter writes to Christians in Asia
64	2 Peter 3:1	Peter apparently writes a second letter to Christians in Asia
64?	1 Tim. 1:3	Paul, apparently after release from prison in Rome, visits Ephesus and leaves Timothy there

64?	Philem. 22	Paul perhaps visits Philemon, Onesimus, and churches in Colossae, Laodicea, and Hierapolis
65	1 Tim. 1:3; Titus 3:12	Paul writes first letter to Timothy at Ephesus possibly from Nicopolis
65	2 Tim. 4:13–15	Paul leaves for Ephesus when he is probably rearrested at Troas
65?	2 Tim. 4:19	Priscilla and Aquila return to Ephesus
65	2 Tim. 4:20	Paul stops at Miletus, where he leaves Trophimus sick
65	2 Tim. 1:15–18; 4:19	Onesiphorus of Ephesus ministers to Paul in Rome, while other believers in Asia desert him
66	2 Tim. 4:12	Paul sends Tychicus to Ephesus with second letter to Timothy
66	2 Tim. 4:13	Timothy brings Paul's cloak and scrolls from Troas to Rome before his martyrdom
67?	Rev. 1:9	John apparently moves to Asia after start of Jewish revolt in Judea
69	Rev. 1:9, 11	John writes Revelation from Patmos to seven churches of Asia (early date)
70s?	John	John writes gospel to Asian Christians
70s–80s?	*Hist. eccl.* 3.31; 5.24	Apostle Philip lives, and is martyred, in Hierapolis
80s?	1 & 2 John	John writes letters to Asian Christians
80s?	3 John	John writes letter to Gaius at Ephesus
90s?	*Adv. Haer.* 3.3.4; *Hist. eccl.* 4.14	Polycarp becomes bishop of Smyrna
90s?	*Adv. Haer.* 5.33	Papias becomes bishop of Hierapolis
95	Rev. 1:9, 11	John writes Revelation from Patmos to seven churches of Asia (late date)

5. Jewish and Christian Apocalypses

Jewish Apocalypses		Christian Apocalypses	
Title	**Date**	**Title**	**Date** (all A.D.)
Book of the Watchers (*1 Enoch* 1–36)	3C B.C.	*Shepherd of Hermas*	1–2C
Book of the Heavenly Luminaries (*1 Enoch* 73–82)	3C B.C.	*Book of Elchasai*	1–2C
Animal Apocalypse (*1 Enoch* 85–90)	2C B.C.	*Ascension of Isaiah* 6–11	1–2C
Apocalypse of Weeks (*1 Enoch* 91:11–17; 93:1–10)	2C B.C.	*Apocalypse of Peter*	2C
Jubilees 23	2C B.C.	*5 Ezra* 2:42–48	2–3C?
Testament of Levi 2–5	2C B.C.	*Jacob's Ladder*	2C?
Testament of Abraham	1C B.C.–A.D. 2C	Testament of the Lord 1:1–14	3C?
Apocalypse of Zephaniah	1C B.C.–A.D. 1C	Questions of Bartholomew	3C?
Similitudes of Enoch (*1 Enoch* 37–71)	A.D. 1C	*Apocalypse of Sedrach*	2–4C?
2 Enoch	A.D. 1C	Apocalypse of Paul	4C
4 Ezra	A.D. 1C	Testament of Isaac	1–5C?
2 Baruch	A.D. 1C	Testament of Jacob	2–5C?
Apocalypse of Abraham	A.D. 1–2C	Story of Zosimus	3–5C
3 Baruch	A.D. 1–2C	Apocalypse of St. John the Theologian	2–9C?
		Book of the Resurrection of Jesus Christ by Bartholomew the Apostle 8b–19b	3–6C?
		Apocalypse of the Virgin Mary	4–9C?
		Apocalypse of the Holy Mother of God Concerning the Punishments	4–11C?
		Apocalypse of Esdras	5–9C?
		Apocalypse of James, the Brother of the Lord	pre-11C
		Mysteries of St. John the Apostle and Holy Virgin	pre-11C

6. Literary Genres of Revelation

Apocalypse	Prophecy	Epistle
Identifies itself as an apocalypse (1:1)	Identifies itself as a prophecy (1:3; 19:10; 22:7, 10, 18, 19)	Identifies author, thus not pseudonymous (1:4, 9; 22:8)
Angelic mediation (1:1; 2:1, 8, 12, 18; 3:1, 7, 14; 17:1–18; 21:9–22:6; 22:8–11)	Use of disclosure language: δείκνυμι ("show"; 1:1; 4:1; 17:1; 21:9, 10; 22:1, 6, 8); σημαίνω ("make known"; 1:1)	Recipients named (1:4)
Epiphany (1:12–20)	Language of fulfillment: ἃ δεῖ γενέσθαι ("what must soon happen"; 1:1; 4:1; 22:6; cf. 1:19)	Epistolary greeting (1:4)
Persecution (2:10, 13; 6:9–11; 7:9, 14; 11:7–10; 12:11; 13:7; 16:6; 18:24; 20:4)	Receives word of God (1:2, 9; 6:9; 20:4)	Body (1:9–22:20)
First-person vision narratives (4:1; 5:1, 2, 6, 11; 6:1, 2; et al.)	Parenesis, or exhortations (1:3; 2:5, 7, 10, 11, 16, 17, 25, 26; 3:2, 3, 5, 8, 10, 11, 12, 19, 21; 12:17; 13:10; 14:12; 16:15; 21:7; 22:7, 9, 11)	Seven "letters" (2:1–3:22)
Future eschatological orientation (1:19; 4:1)	Suffering in exile (1:9)	Epistolary closing (22:21)
Visions (4:2–22:6)	Prophetic experiences "in the Spirit" (1:10; 4:2; 17:3; 21:10)	
Otherworldly journey (4:1)	Commanded to write (1:11, 19; 2:1, 8, 12, 18; 3:1, 7, 14; 14:13; 19:9; 21:5)	
Otherworldly writing (5:1–6:17; 8:1; 10:2, 8–11)	Present historical orientation (1:19)	
Dialogue (7:13–17; 17:6b–18)	Use of Τάδε λέγει ("Thus says . . .") declaration formula (2:1, 8, 12, 18; 3:1, 7, 14)	
Auditions (11:15–18; 14:2–3, 13; 19:1–8)	Heavenly throne room vision (4:1–2)	
Discourse (21:5–8)	Prophets mentioned (10:7; 11:10, 18; 16:6; 18:20, 24; 22:6, 9)	
	Prophetic commission (10:8–11)	
	Prophetic act (11:1–2)	
	Prophetic journey (17:1; 21:10)	
	Prophetic oath formula (19:9; 21:5; 22:6, 18)	
	Prophetic seal (22:10)	
	Prophetic curse (22:18–19)	

7. Chapter and Verse Counts with Text Set as Poetry

Chapters	Verses	UBS[4]	NIV	NKJV
22	405	53 verses	51 verses	16 verses
1	20	1:7	1:7	
2	29	2:26–27	2:27	2:27
3	22	3:7		
4	11	4:8, 11	4:8, 11	4:8, 11
5	14	5:9–10, 12, 13	5:9–10, 12, 13	5:9–10, 12, 13
6	17			
7	17	7:10, 12, 15–17	7:10, 12, 15–17	7:12
8	13			
9	21			
10	11	10:5–6		
11	19	11:15, 17–18	11:15, 17–18	11:17–18
12	17	12:10–12	12:10–12	
13	18	13:10	13:10	
14	20			
15	8	15:3–4	15:3–4	15:3–4
16	21	16:5–6, 7	16:5–6, 7	16:5–6
17	18		17:5	17:5
18	24	18:2–3, 4–8, 10, 14, 16, 19–20, 21–24	18:2–3, 4–8, 10, 16–17, 19–20, 21–24	
19	21	19:1–2, 3, 4, 5, 6–8	19:1–2, 3, 4, 5, 6–8, 16	19:16
20	15			
21	27			
22	21			

8. Words Occurring Only in Revelation
(Hapax Legomena)

Verse	Hapax	NRSV (unless noted)
1:8; 21:6; 22:13	ἄλφα	Alpha
1:8; 21:6; 22:13	ὦ	Omega
1:13	ποδήρης	long robe
1:15; 2:18	χαλκολίβανον	burnished bronze
2:23	νεφρός	mind
2:27	κεραμικός	clay
2:28; 22:16	πρωϊνός	morning
3:15 (2x), 16	ζεστός	hot
3:16	χλιαρὸς	lukewarm
3:16	ἐμέω	to spit out
3:18	κολλ[ο]ύριον	salve
3:18	ἐγχρίω	to anoint
3:19	ζηλεύω	to be earnest
4:3	σμαράγδινος	emerald
4:3, 4, 8	κυκλόθεν	around
4:3; 10:1	ἶρις	rainbow
4:3; 21:11, 18, 19	ἴασπις	jasper
4:3; 21:20	σάρδιον	carnelian
4:6; 15:2	ὑάλινος	of glass
4:6; 22:1	κρύσταλλος	crystal
4:7; 8:13; 12:14; 14:6; 19:17	πέτομαι	to fly
5:1	κατεσφραγίζω	to seal
5:8; 15:7; 16:1, 2, 3, 4, 8, 10, 12, 17; 17:1; 21:9	φιάλη	bowl
6:2	τόξον	bow
6:4; 12:3	πυρρός	bright red
6:6 (2x)	χοῖνιξ	quart
6:6	κριθή	barley
6:9; 9:1; 16:10; 21:20	πέμπτος	fifth
6:12	τρίχινος	of hair (NKJV)
6:13	ὄλυνθος	late figs (NIV)
7:3; 9:4; 13:16; 14:1, 9; 17:5; 20:4; 22:4	μέτωπον	forehead
7:16; 16:9	καῦμα	scorching heat
8:1	ἡμιώριον	half an hour
8:3, 5	λιβανωτός	censer
8:7; 11:19; 16:21 (2x)	χάλαζα	hail

8:12	πλήσσω	to strike
8:13; 14:6; 19:17	μεσουράνημα	midheaven
9:5 (2x); 14:11; 18:7, 10, 15	βασανισμός	torture
9:10 (2x), 19 (2x); 12:4	οὐρά	tail
9:16	ἱππικός	cavalry
9:16	δισμυριάς	twenty thousand [20,000 x 10,000 = 200 million]
9:17	πύρινος	color of fire
9:17	ὑακίνθινος	[color of] sapphire
9:17	θειώδης	[color of] sulfur
9:20	χαλκοῦς	bronze
9:21	κλέμμα	theft
10:2, 9, 10	βιβλαρίδιον	little scroll
10:3	μυκάομαι	to roar
12:3, 4, 7 (2x), 9, 13, 16, 17; 13:2, 4, 11; 16:13; 20:2	δράκων	dragon
12:3; 13:1; 19:12	διάδημα	diadem
12:10	κατήγωρ	accuser
12:15	ποταμοφόρητος	sweep away with the flood
13:2	πάρδαλις	leopard
13:2	ἄρκος	bear
13:18; 14:20	ἑξακόσιοι	six hundred
14:2; 18:22	κιθαρῳδός	harpist
14:10	ἄκρατος	unmixed
14:10; 18:6	κεράννυμι	to pour
14:18	ἀκμάζω	to be ripe
14:18	βότρυς	cluster
16:10	μασάομαι	to gnaw
16:13	βάτραχος	frog
16:21	ταλαντιαῖος	weighing about a hundred pounds
17:4; 18:16	χρυσοῦς	gold
18:2; 19:17, 21	ὄρνεον	bird
18:3	στρῆνος	luxury
18:6	διπλόω	double
18:7, 9	στρηνιάω	to live in luxury
18:12	βύσσινος	fine linen
18:12	σιρικός	silk
18:12	θύϊνος	scented wood
18:12	ἐλεφάντινος	of ivory
18:12	μάρμαρος	marble
18:13	κιννάμωμον	cinnamon
18:13	ἄμωμον	spice

18:13	σεμίδαλις	choice flour
18:13	ῥέδη	chariot
18:14	ὀπώρα	fruit
18:14	διπαρός	dainties; luxuries (NLT)
18:19	τιμιότης	wealth
18:21	μύλινος	millstone
18:21	ὅρμημα	violence
18:22	μουσικός	musician (NIV)
18:22	σαλπιστής	trumpeter
19:1, 3, 4, 6	ἀλληλουϊά	hallelujah
19:16	μηρός	thigh
20:4	πελεκίζω	to behead
20:9	κυκλεύω	surround
21:8; 22:15	φάρμακος	sorcerer
21:11	κρυσταλλίζω	to be clear as crystal
21:16	τετράγωνος	foursquare
21:18	ἐνδώμησις	construction (NKJV)
21:18, 21	ὕαλος	glass
21:19	σάπφιρος	sapphire
21:19	χαλκηδών	agate; chalcedony (NIV)
21:19	σμάραγδος	emerald
21:20	σαρδόνυξ	onyx; sardonyx (NIV)
21:20	χρυσόλιθος	chrysolite
21:20	βήρυλλος	beryl
21:20	τοπάζιον	topaz
21:20	χρυσόπρασος	chrysoprase
21:20	ὑακίνθος	jacinth
21:20	δωδέκατος	twelfth
21:20	ἀμέθυστος	amethyst
21:21	διαυγής	transparent
22:3	κατάθεμα	accursed
22:11	ῥυπαίνομαι	to be filthy

9. Allusions and Verbal Parallels in the
Old Testament and Extrabiblical Literature

Revelation	Old Testament and Extrabiblical Literature
1:1	Dan. 2:28, 29, 45
1:4	Exod. 3:14; Isa. 41:4
1:5	Pss. 89:27; 130:8; Isa. 40:2
1:6	Exod. 19:6; Isa. 61:6
1:7	Dan. 7:13; Zech. 12:10, 12, 14
1:8	Exod. 3:14; Isa. 41:4; Amos 3:13 LXX; 4:13 LXX
1:13	Ezek. 9:2, 11 LXX; Dan. 7:13; 10:5
1:14	Dan. 7:9
1:14–15	Dan. 10:6
1:15	Ezek. 1:24; 43:2
1:16	Isa. 49:2
1:17	Isa. 44:6; 48:12
1:19	Isa. 48:6 LXX; Dan. 2:28, 29, 45
2:6	Ps. 139:21
2:7	Gen. 2:8 LXX, 2:9; 3:22, 24; Ezek. 28:13 LXX; 31:8, 9 LXX
2:8	Isa. 44:6; 48:12
2:10	Dan. 1:12, 14
2:12	Isa. 49:2
2:14	Num. 25:1–2; 31:16
2:16	Isa. 49:2
2:17	Ps. 78:24; Isa. 62:2; 65:15
2:18	Dan. 10:6
2:20	Num. 25:1–2; 1 Kings 16:31; 2 Kings 9:22
2:23	Pss. 7:9; 62:12; Prov. 24:12; Jer. 11:20; 17:10
2:26–27	Ps. 2:8, 9; *Pss. Sol.* 17:23–24
3:5	Exod. 32:32, 33; Ps. 69:28; Dan. 12:1
3:7	Job 12:14; Isa. 22:22
3:9	Isa. 43:4; 45:14; 49:23; 60:14
3:12	Isa. 62:2; 65:15; Ezek. 48:35
3:14	Prov. 8:22
3:17	Hos. 12:8
3:19	Prov. 3:12
4:1	Exod. 19:20, 24; Dan. 2:28, 29, 45
4:2	1 Kings 22:19; 2 Chron. 18:18; Ps. 47:8; Isa. 6:1; Ezek. 1:26–27; Sir. 1:8
4:3	Ezek. 1:26–28
4:4	Isa. 24:23
4:5	Exod. 19:16; Esther 1:1d LXX; Ezek. 1:13; Zech. 4:2

4:6	Ezek. 1:22
4:6–7	Ezek. 1:5–10; 10:14
4:8	Exod. 3:14; Isa. 6:2, 3; 41:4; Ezek. 1:18; 10:12; Amos 3:13 LXX; 4:13 LXX
4:9	1 Kings 22:19; 2 Chron. 18:18; Ps. 47:8; Isa. 6:1; Ezek. 1:26–27; Dan. 4:34; 6:26; 12:7; Sir. 1:8
4:10	1 Kings 22:19; 2 Chron. 18:18; Ps. 47:8; Isa. 6:1; Ezek. 1:26–27; Sir. 1:8
5:1	1 Kings 22:19; 2 Chron. 18:18; Ps. 47:8; Isa. 6:1; 29:11; Ezek. 1:26–27; 2:9–10; Sir. 1:8
5:5	Gen. 49:9–10; Isa. 11:1, 10
5:6	Isa. 53:7; Zech. 4:10
5:7	1 Kings 22:19; 2 Chron. 18:18; Ps. 47:8; Isa. 6:1; Ezek. 1:26–27; Sir. 1:8
5:8	Ps. 141:2
5:9	Pss. 33:3; 40:3; 96:1; 98:1; 144:9; 149:1; Isa. 42:10
5:10	Exod. 19:6; Isa. 61:6
5:11	Dan. 7:10; *1 En.* 14:22
5:12	1 Chron. 29:11; Isa. 53:7
5:13	1 Kings 22:19; 2 Chron. 18:18; Ps. 47:8; Isa. 6:1; Ezek. 1:26–27; Sir. 1:8
6:2	Zech. 1:8; 6:3, 6
6:4	Zech. 1:8; 6:2
6:5	Zech. 6:2, 6
6:8	Jer. 14:12; 15:3; Ezek. 5:12, 17; 14:21; 33:27
6:10	Deut. 32:43; 2 Kings 9:7; Ps. 79:10
6:12	Joel 2:31
6:12–13	Isa. 13:10; Ezek. 32:7, 8; Joel 2:10; 3:15
6:13–14	Isa. 34:4
6:15	Isa. 2:10, 19, 21; Jer. 4:29
6:16	1 Kings 22:19; 2 Chron. 18:18; Ps. 47:8; Isa. 6:1; Ezek. 1:26–27; Hos. 10:8; Sir. 1:8
6:17	Joel 2:11; Nah. 1:6; Mal. 3:2
7:1	Jer. 49:36; Ezek. 37:9; Dan. 7:2; Zech. 6:5
7:3	Ezek. 9:4
7:10	1 Kings 22:19; 2 Chron. 18:18; Ps. 47:8; Isa. 6:1; Ezek. 1:26–27; Sir. 1:8
7:14	Dan. 12:1
7:15	1 Kings 22:19; 2 Chron. 18:18; Ps. 47:8; Isa. 6:1; Ezek. 1:26–27; Sir. 1:8
7:16	Isa. 49:10
7:17	Ps. 23:1, 2; Isa. 25:8; 49:10; Jer. 2:13; Ezek. 34:23
8:3	Exod. 30:1–3; Ps. 141:2
8:4	Ps. 141:2
8:5	Exod. 19:16–19; Lev. 16:12; Esther 1:1d LXX
8:7	Exod. 9:23–25; Ezek. 38:22; Wis. 16:22
8:8	Exod. 7:20, 21
8:11	Jer. 9:15
8:12	Isa. 13:10; Ezek. 32:7, 8; Joel 2:10; 3:15
9:2	Gen. 19:28; Exod. 19:18
9:3	Exod. 10:12, 15; Wis. 16:9

9:6	Job 3:21; Jer. 8:3; Hos. 10:8
9:7	Joel 2:4, 5
9:8	Joel 1:6
9:9	Joel 2:5
9:13	Exod. 30:1–3
9:20	Deut. 32:17; Pss. 115:4–7; 135:15–17; Dan. 5:23
10:4	Dan. 8:26; 12:4, 9
10:5–6	Deut. 32:40; Dan. 12:7
10:6	Gen. 14:19, 22; Exod. 20:11; Neh. 9:6; Ps. 146:6
10:7	Dan. 9:6, 10; Amos 3:7; Zech. 1:6
10:9–10	Ezek. 2:8; 3:1–3
10:11	Jer. 1:10; 25:30; Dan. 3:4; 7:14
11:1	Ezek. 40:3; Zech. 2:1–2
11:2	Ps. 79:1; Isa. 63:18; Zech. 12:3 LXX
11:4	Zech. 4:3, 11–14
11:5	2 Sam. 22:9; 2 Kings 1:10; Ps. 97:3; Jer. 5:14
11:6	Exod. 7:17, 19–20; 1 Sam. 4:8; 1 Kings 17:1
11:7	Dan. 7:3, 7, 21
11:8	Isa. 1:10
11:11	Ezek. 37:5, 10
11:12	2 Kings 2:11
11:13	Ezek. 38:19–20
11:15	Exod. 15:18; Pss. 10:16; 22:28; Dan. 2:44; 7:14; Obad. 21; Zech. 14:9
11:17	Exod. 3:14; Amos 3:13 LXX; 4:13 LXX
11:18	Pss. 2:1; 46:6; 115:13; Dan. 9:6, 10; Amos 3:7; Zech. 1:6
11:19	Exod. 9:24; 19:16; 1 Kings 8:1, 6; 2 Chron. 5:7; Esther 1:1d LXX; Ezek. 1:13
12:2	Isa. 66:7; Mic. 4:10
12:3	Dan. 7:7
12:4	Dan. 8:10
12:5	Ps. 2:9; Isa. 7:14; 66:7
12:7	Dan. 10:13, 21; 12:1
12:9	Isa. 14:12
12:10	Job 1:9–11; Zech. 3:1
12:14	Dan. 7:25; 12:7
12:17	Dan. 7:7, 21
13:1	Dan. 7:3
13:2	Dan. 7:4–6
13:5	Dan. 7:8, 20, 25; 11:36
13:7	Dan. 7:7, 21
13:8	Exod. 32:32, 33; Ps. 69:28; Isa. 53:7; Dan. 12:1
13:10	Jer. 15:2; 43:11
13:13	1 Kings 18:24–39

13:14	Deut. 13:2–4
13:15	Dan. 3:5–6
14:1	Ezek. 9:4
14:2	Ezek. 1:24; 43:2
14:3	Pss. 33:3; 40:3; 96:1; 98:1; 144:9; 149:1; Isa. 42:10
14:5	Ps. 32:2; Isa. 53:9; Zeph. 3:13
14:7	Exod. 20:11; Ps. 146:6
14:8	Isa. 21:9; Jer. 51:7, 8
14:10	Gen. 19:24; Pss. 11:6; 75:8; Isa. 51:17, 22; Jer. 25:15; Ezek. 38:22; 3 Macc. 2:5
14:11	Isa. 34:10
14:14	Dan. 7:13
14:15	Joel 3:13
14:18	Joel 3:13
14:20	Isa. 63:3; Lam. 1:15
15:1	Lev. 26:21
15:3	Exod. 15:1, 11; Deut. 32:4; Pss. 92:5; 111:2; 139:14; 145:17; Jer. 10:10 Theodotion; Amos 3:13 LXX; 4:13 LXX; *1 En.* 9:4; 25:5; 27:3; Tob. 13:7, 11
15:4	Ps. 86:9; Jer. 10:6–7; Mal. 1:11
15:5	Exod. 38:21; 40:34
15:6	Lev. 26:21
15:7	Ps. 75:8; Isa. 51:17, 22; Jer. 25:15
15:8	Exod. 40:34; 1 Kings 8:10–11; 2 Chron. 5:13–14; Isa. 6:4; Ezek. 44:4
16:1	Ps. 69:24; Isa. 66:6; Jer. 10:25; Ezek. 22:31; Zeph. 3:8
16:2	Exod. 9:10; Deut. 28:35
16:3	Exod. 7:17–21
16:4	Exod. 7:19–24; Ps. 78:44
16:5	Exod. 3:14; Deut. 32:4; Pss. 119:137; 145:17
16:6	Ps. 79:3; Isa. 49:26
16:7	Pss. 19:9; 119:137; Amos 3:13 LXX; 4:13 LXX
16:10	Exod. 10:21; Isa. 8:22
16:12	Isa. 11:15; 44:27; Jer. 50:38; 51:36
16:14	Amos 3:13 LXX; 4:13 LXX
16:16	Judg. 5:19; 2 Kings 9:27; 23:29; Zech. 12:11
16:17	Isa. 66:6
16:18	Exod. 19:16–19; Esther 1:1d LXX; Dan. 12:1
16:19	Ps. 75:8; Isa. 51:17, 22; Jer. 25:15
16:21	Exod. 9:24
17:1	Jer. 51:13
17:2	Isa. 23:17; Jer. 51:7
17:4	Jer. 51:7; Ezek. 28:13
17:8	Exod. 32:32, 33; Ps. 69:28; Dan. 7:3; 12:1
17:12	Dan. 7:24

17:14	Deut. 10:17; Dan. 2:47; *1 En.* 9:4; 2 Macc. 13:4; 3 Macc. 5:35
17:16	Lev. 21:9
18:2	Isa. 13:21; 21:9; 34:11; Jer. 50:39; 51:8; Bar. 4:35
18:3	Isa. 23:17; Jer. 51:7
18:4	Isa. 48:20; 52:11; Jer. 50:8; 51:6, 9, 45
18:5	Gen. 18:20, 21; Jer. 51:9
18:6	Ps. 137:8; Jer. 50:15, 29
18:7–8	Isa. 47:7–9
18:8	Lev. 21:9; Jer. 50:34
18:9	Ezek. 26:16; 27:30–35
18:10	Ezek. 26:17; Dan. 4:30
18:11	Ezek. 27:36
18:12–13	Ezek. 27:12, 13, 22
18:15	Ezek. 27:36
18:16	Ezek. 28:13
18:17	Ezek. 27:27–29
18:18	Ezek. 27:32
18:19	Ezek. 27:30–34
18:20	Deut. 23:43 LXX; Ps. 96:11; Isa. 44:23; 49:13; Jer. 51:48
18:21	Jer. 51:63–64; Ezek. 26:21
18:22	Isa. 24:8; Ezek. 26:13
18:23	Isa. 23:8; 47:9; Jer. 7:34; 16:9; Jer. 25:10
18:24	Jer. 51:49; Ezek. 24:7
19:1	Tob. 13:18
19:2	Deut. 32:43; 2 Kings 9:7; Pss. 19:9; 79:10; 119:137
19:3	Isa. 34:10
19:4	1 Kings 22:19; 2 Chron. 18:18; Ps. 47:8; Isa. 6:1; Ezek. 1:26–27; Sir. 1:8
19:5	Pss. 22:23; 115:13; 134:1; 135:1
19:6	Exod. 15:18; Pss. 22:28; 93:1; 97:1; 99:1; Ezek. 1:24; 43:2; Dan. 7:14; Amos 3:13 LXX; 4:13 LXX; Zech. 14:9
19:8	Isa. 61:10
19:11	Ps. 96:13; Isa. 11:4; Ezek. 1:1; Zech. 1:8; 6:3, 6
19:12	Dan. 10:6
19:13	Isa. 63:1–3
19:15	Ps. 2:9; Isa. 49:2; 63:3; Lam. 1:15; Joel 3:13; Amos 3:13 LXX; 4:13 LXX
19:16	Deut. 10:17; Dan. 2:47; *1 En.* 9:4; 2 Macc. 13:4; 3 Macc. 5:35
19:17–18	Ezek. 39:17–20
19:19	Ps. 2:2
19:20	Isa. 30:33
19:21	Ezek. 39:17, 20
20:4	Dan. 7:9, 22, 27
20:6	Exod. 19:6; Isa. 61:6

20:8	Ezek. 7:2; 38:2
20:9	2 Kings 1:10; Ezek. 38:22; 39:6
20:10	Gen. 19:24; Ps. 11:6; Isa. 30:33; Ezek. 38:22; 3 Macc. 2:5
20:11	Ps. 114:3–7
20:11–12	Dan. 7:9–10
20:12	Exod. 32:32, 33; Ps. 69:28; Dan. 12:1
20:12–13	Pss. 28:4; 62:12; Prov. 24:12; Isa. 59:18; Jer. 17:10
20:15	Exod. 32:32, 33; Ps. 69:28; Isa. 30:33; Dan. 12:1
21:1	Isa. 65:17; 66:22
21:2	Isa. 52:1; 61:10
21:3	Lev. 26:11–12; 2 Chron. 6:18; Ezek. 37:27; Zech. 2:10
21:4	Isa. 25:8; 35:10; 65:19
21:5	1 Kings 22:19; 2 Chron. 18:18; Ps. 47:8; Isa. 6:1; Ezek. 1:26–27; Sir. 1:8
21:6	Ps. 36:9; Isa. 44:6; 48:12; 55:1; Jer. 2:13
21:7	2 Sam. 7:14
21:8	Gen. 19:24; Ps. 11:6; Isa. 30:33; Ezek. 38:22; 3 Macc. 2:5
21:10	Ezek. 40:2
21:11	Isa. 60:1, 2, 19
21:12–13	Exod. 28:21; Ezek. 48:30–35
21:15	Ezek. 40:3, 5
21:16–17	Ezek. 48:16, 17
21:19	Isa. 54:11–12
21:22	Amos 3:13 LXX; 4:13 LXX
21:23	Isa. 60:19–20
21:24	Isa. 60:3, 5; *Pss. Sol.* 17:31
21:25	Isa. 60:11; Zech. 14:7
21:26	Ps. 72:10–11; *Pss. Sol.* 17:31
21:27	Exod. 32:32, 33; Ps. 69:28; Isa. 52:1; Dan. 12:1
22:1	Ezek. 47:1; Joel 3:18; Zech. 14:8
22:2	Gen. 2:9; 3:22; Ezek. 47:12
22:3	Zech. 14:11
22:4	Pss. 17:15; 42:2
22:5	Isa. 60:19–20; Dan. 7:18, 27; Zech. 14:7
22:6	Dan. 2:28, 29, 45
22:10	Dan. 12:4
22:12	Pss. 28:4; 62:12; Prov. 24:12; Isa. 40:10; 59:18; 62:11; Jer. 17:10
22:13	Isa. 44:6; 48:12
22:14	Gen. 2:9; 3:22; Ezek. 47:12
22:16	Num. 24:17; Isa. 11:1, 10
22:17	Isa. 55:1
22:18–19	Deut. 4:2; 12:32
22:19	Gen. 2:9; 3:22; Ezek. 47:12

10. Structure of Revelation

Threefold Structure Based on 1:19

    I.   What You Have Seen (1:1–20)
   II.   What Is Now (2:1–3:21)
 III. What Will Take Place Later (4:1–22:21)

Fourfold Structure Based on "In the Spirit" Experiences

    I.   In the Spirit on the Island of Patmos (1:9–10)
   II.   In the Spirit in Heaven (4:1–2)
 III. In the Spirit in a Desert (17:3)
 IV. In the Spirit on a Mountain (21:10)

Chiastic Structure

A   Prologue and Greeting (1:1–8)
      B   Seven Churches (1:4–4:2)
           C   Seven Seals (3:21–8:5)
                 D   Seven Trumpets–Angels–Two Witnesses (8:2–11:19)
                       E   Woman, Dragon, and Male Child (12:1–17)
                 D' Two Beasts–Angels–Seven Bowls (13:1–16:21)
           C' Destruction of Babylon (16:18–19:10)
      B' New Jerusalem, the Bride (19:6–22:9)
A' Closing and Epilogue (22:6–21)

Sevenfold Drama Structure

Prologue (1:1–8)
Act 1   The Seven Golden Lampstands (1:9–3:22)
Act 2   The Seven Seals (4:1–8:4)
Act 3   The Seven Trumpets (8:5–11:18)
Act 4   The Seven Tableaux (11:19–15:4)
Act 5   The Seven Bowls of Wrath (15:5–16:21)
Act 6   The Seven Judgments (17:1–20:3)
Act 7   The Seven Great Promises (20:4–22:5)
Epilogue (22:6–21)

11. Identification of Christ with God in Revelation

A	B	B'	A'
1:8	1:17	21:6	22:13
Prologue	First vision	Last vision	Epilogue
God	Christ	God	Christ
Alpha and Omega		Alpha and Omega	Alpha and Omega
	First and Last		First and Last
		Beginning and End	Beginning and End
One who is to come (cf. 1:7)			He is coming soon (22:12; cf. 7, 20)
	Connection with eternal life (1:18)	Connection with eternal life	

12. Divine Names in Revelation

God	References
God	83 times (occurs in every chapter)
One who is and was and is to come	1:4, 8; 4:8
One who is and was	11:17; 16:5
Father	1:6; 2:27; 3:5, 21; 14:1
Alpha and Omega	1:8; 21:6
Almighty	1:8; 16:14; 19:15
Lord God Almighty	4:8; 11:17; 15:3; 16:7; 19:6; 21:22
Lord (and) God	1:8; 4:11; 18:8; 22:5, 6
Lord	11:15; 15:4
Him who sits on the throne	4:9–10; 5:13; 7:10; 19:4
Sovereign Lord	6:10
Holy and true	6:10
Living God	7:2; 15:7
God of heaven	11:13; 16:11
King of the nations (NIV, REB: King of the ages; KJV, NKJV: King of the saints)	15:3
Holy One	16:5
Beginning and end	21:6

Holy Spirit	References
Sevenfold Spirit/seven spirits (of God)	1:4; 3:1; 4:5; 5:6
Spirit	1:10; 2:7, 11, 17, 29; 3:6, 13, 22; 4:2; 14:13; 17:3; 21:10; 22:17
s(S)pirit of life?	11:11
Spirit of (the) prophecy	19:10

Jesus Christ	References
Jesus Christ	1:1, 2, 5
Jesus	1:9 (2x); 12:17; 14:12; 17:6; 19:10 (2x); 20:4; 22:16
Lord Jesus	22:20, 21
Faithful (and true) witness; Faithful and True	1:5; 3:14; 19:11
Firstborn from the dead	1:5
Ruler of the kings of the earth	1:5
Son of Man	1:13; 14:14
Him who holds seven stars in his right hand	1:16; 2:1
First and last	1:17; 2:8; 22:13
Living One	1:18
Him who walks among the seven golden lampstands	2:1
Him who holds the sharp, double-edged sword	2:12

Son of God	2:18
Him who holds the sevenfold Spirit of God and the seven stars	3:1
Holy and true One	3:7
Him who holds the key of David	3:7
Amen	3:14
Beginning of God's creation	3:14
Lion of the tribe of Judah	5:5
Root (and offspring) of David	5:5; 22:16
Lamb	5:6, 8, 12, 13; 6:1, 16; 7:9, 10, 14, 17; 12:11; 13:8, 11; 14:1, 4 (2x), 10; 15:3; 17:14 (2x); 19:7, 9; 21:9, 14, 22, 23, 27; 22:1, 3
Christ	11:15; 12:10; 20:4, 6
Male child	12:5, 13
Lord (of lords)	14:13; 17:14; 19:16
King of kings	17:14; 19:16
Word of God	19:13
Alpha and the Omega	22:13
Beginning and the end	22:13
Bright morning star	22:16

13. Names for Believers in Revelation

Name	On Earth	In Heaven
Servants	1:1; 2:20; 7:3; 10:7; 11:18; 15:3; 19:2; 22:6	19:5; 22:3
Fellow servants	6:11; 19:10; 22:9	6:11
One who reads of the words of the prophecy	1:3	
Those who hear (the words)	1:3; 22:8, 17, 18	
Those who keep the words/commandments	1:3; 2:26; 12:17; 14:12; 16:15; 22:7, 9	
Kingdom	1:6; 5:10	
Priests	1:6; 5:10	20:6
Brothers	1:9; 6:11; 12:10; 19:10; 22:9	6:11
Partner in tribulation	1:9	
Church(es)	1:4, 11, 20; 2:1, 7, 8, 11, 12, 17, 18, 23, 29; 3:1, 6, 7, 13, 14, 22; 22:16	
Apostles	2:2	18:20; 21:14
Those who have an ear	2:7, 11, 17, 29; 3:6, 13, 22; 13:9	
Those who are victorious	2:7, 11, 17, 26; 3:5, 12, 21; 21:7	15:2
Faithful witness	2:13	
Witness(es)	11:3; 22:20	
One who is watchful	16:15; cf. 3:2	
Saints	5:8; 8:3, 4; 11:18; 13:7, 10; 14:12; 16:6; 17:6; 18:24; 19:8; 20:9; 22:11, [21]	18:20
Souls who were slaughtered/beheaded	18:24	6:9; 20:4
Those who were sealed	7:4, 5, 8	cf. 14:1
144,000	7:4	14:1, 3
Tribe(s) of Israel	7:4, 5, 6, 7, 8	21:12
Great multitude		7:9; 19:1, 6
Prophets	10:7; 11:10, 18; 16:6; 18:24; 22:6, 9	18:20
Those who fear him or his name	11:18	19:5
Offspring of the woman	12:17	
Virgins		14:4
Those who follow the Lamb		14:4
Firstfruits		14:4
My people	18:4	
Wife		19:7; 21:9
Holy City		21:2, 10
New Jerusalem		21:2, 10
Bride		21:2, 9; 22:17
My son	21:7	
Righteous one	22:11	

14. Apocalyptic Themes in Revelation, the Synoptic Gospels, and Pauline Epistles

Theme	Revelation	Synoptic Gospels	Pauline Epistles
Ruling the nations	1:5; 2:26–27; 12:5; 19:15	Matt. 2:6	Rom. 15:12
Coming with the clouds	1:7	Matt. 24:30; Mark 13:26; Luke 21:27	1 Thess. 4:17
Every eye will see him	1:7	Matt. 24:30; Mark 13:26; Luke 21:27	
All tribes of earth will mourn	1:7	Matt. 24:30	
Suffering by synagogues	2:9–10; 3:9 ("of Satan")	Mark 13:9; Luke 21:12	2 Cor. 11:24; 1 Thess. 2:14
Promise of a crown	2:10; 3:11		1 Cor. 9:25; 1 Thess. 2:19; 2 Tim. 4:8
Reference "to the end"	2:26	Matt. 10:22; 24:13; Mark 13:13	1 Cor. 1:8
Exhortation to keep awake	3:2, 3; 16:15	Matt. 24:42; 25:13; Mark 13:35, 37; Luke 12:37	Rom. 13:11; 1 Thess. 5:6
Lord's coming as a thief	3:3; 16:15	Matt. 24:43; Luke 12:39	1 Thess. 5:2, 4
Be dressed for service	3:4–5; 16:15; 19:14; 21:2	Luke 12:35, 37	
Book of Life	3:5; 13:8; 17:8; 20:12, 15; 21:27		Phil. 4:3
Heavenly Jerusalem	3:12; 21:2, 10		Gal. 4:26
Saints will reign	5:10; 20:6; 22:5		2 Tim. 2:12
Time of vengeance	6:10; 11:18; 19:2	Luke 18:7–8; 21:22	Rom. 12:19; 1 Thess. 4:6; 2 Thess. 1:8–9
Example of fig tree	6:13	Matt. 24:32; Mark 13:28; Luke 21:29	
Earth's inhabitants fearful	6:15	Luke 21:26	
Call to mountains to "fall on us"	6:16	Luke 23:30	
Day of wrath	6:16–17; 16:19; 19:15	Luke 21:23	Rom. 2:5; Col. 3:6; 1 Thess. 1:10
Angels and four winds	7:1	Matt. 24:31; Mark 13:27	
Saints stand before Jesus	7:9	Luke 21:36	
Great tribulation	7:14	Matt. 24:21; Mark 13:19–20	
Angel sounds final trumpet	10:7; 11:15	Matt. 24:31	1 Cor. 15:52; 1 Thess. 4:16
Jerusalem to be trampled by Gentiles	11:2–3	Luke 21:24	
Servants receive heavenly reward	11:18; 22:12	Matt. 5:12; 6:1; 16:27; Luke 6:23	1 Cor. 3:14; Eph. 6:8; Col. 3:24
Deceiving the nations	12:9; 13:14; 18:23; 19:20; 20:3, 8, 10	Matt. 24:4–5, 11; Mark 13:5–6; Luke 21:8	2 Thess. 2:3; 1 Tim. 4:1

Killed by a sword	13:10; cf. 20:4	Luke 21:24	
Exhortation to endurance	13:10; 14:12	Luke 21:19	Rom. 8:25
False signs and wonders	13:13–14; 16:14; 19:20	Matt. 24:24; Mark 13:22	2 Thess. 2:9
Gospel to be preached	14:6	Matt. 24:14; Mark 13:10	
Fire in final judgment	14:10–11; 19:20; 20:14–15; 21:8	Matt. 3:12; 5:22; 13:40, 42, 50; 18:8–9; 25:41; Mark 9:43, 48; Luke 3:17; 16:24	1 Cor. 3:13, 15; 2 Thess. 1:7
Lord's coming preceded by a shout	14:15, 18; 19:17		1 Thess. 4:16
Judgment as a harvest	14:15–16	Matt. 3:12; 13:39	
Angels involved in judgment	14:17–19	Matt. 13:49; 24:31; Mark 13:27	2 Thess. 1:7
Appearance of False Prophet	16:13; 19:20; 20:10	Matt. 24:11, 24; Mark 13:22	
Drunkenness portrayed negatively	17:2	Matt. 24:49; Luke 21:34	1 Thess. 5:7
Warning against abominations	17:4–5; cf. 21:27	Matt. 24:15; Mark 13:14	
The elect with Jesus	17:14	Matt. 24:31; Mark 13:27	
Exhortation to come out and flee	18:4	Matt. 24:16; Mark 13:14; Luke 21:21	
Destruction eternal	19:3; 20:10		2 Thess. 1:9
Final messianic banquet	19:9	Matt. 8:11; Luke 14:15; 22:30	
Messiah conquers with his mouth	19:15, 21		2 Thess. 2:8
Saints to judge from thrones	20:4; cf. 3:21	Matt. 19:28; Luke 22:30	
Dead appear for judgment	20:12–13	Matt. 10:15; 11:22, 24; 12:36, 41–42; Luke 10:14; 11:31–32	Rom. 14:10; 2 Cor. 5:10
Death destroyed	20:14		1 Cor. 15:26
Heaven and earth pass away	21:1	Matt. 24:35; Mark 13:31; Luke 21:33	

15. Thematic Parallels Between Revelation and John

	Revelation	John
Christy		
Witness	1:2, 5, 9; 3:14; 12:17; 19:10; 22:16, 20	3:11, 32–33; 5:31, 36; 7:7; 8:13–14; 13:21; 18:37
Atoning blood	1:5; 5:9; 7:14; 12:11	6:53–56
I am (ἐγώ εἰμι)	1:8, 17; 21:6; 22:16	6:35, 41, 48, 51; 8:12, 24, 28; 9:5; 10:7, 9, 11, 14; 11:25; 13:19; 14:6; 15:1, 5
Victor	3:21; 5:5; 17:14; 19:11	16:33
Unity with God	3:21; 5:6; 7:10, 17; 14:4; 20:6; 21:22–23; 22:1, 3	10:30–38; 14:7–11; 15:23–24; 17:3, 5, 10–13, 21–23
Lamb	5:6, 8, 12, 13; 6:1, 16; 7:9, 10, 14, 17; 12:11; 13:8; 14:1, 4 (2x), 10; 15:3; 17:14; 19:7, 9; 21:9, 14, 22, 23, 27; 22:1, 3 (ἀρνίον)	1:29, 36 (ἀμνός)
Shepherd	7:17	10:11, 14, 16
Judge	19:11	5:22, 27, 30; 8:16; 9:39
Word	19:13	1:1, 14; cf. 1 John 1:1
Temple	21:22	2:19, 21
Holy Spirit		
Speaks to congregation	2:7, 11, 17, 29; 3:6, 13, 22; 14:13	14:26; 16:13, 15
Witness of Jesus	19:10	15:26
Angels		
Servants of God	1:20; 2:1, 8, 12, 18; 3:1, 7, 14; 22:6, 16	1:51
Live in heaven	5:11; 8:2; 12:7; 15:1, 6–7; 16:1	1:51
Satan		
Devil	2:10; 12:9, 12; 20:2, 10	8:44; 13:2
Ruler and general	12:7–12; 19:19–21; 20:7–10	12:31; 14:30; 16:11
Church		
Witnesses	1:2, 9; 2:13; 6:9; 12:11, 17; 17:6; 19:10; 20:4	1:7–8, 19; 4:39; 15:27; 19:35; 21:24
Hates evil	2:6	12:25
True Jews	2:9; 3:9	4:23; 8:31, 39–44
Characterized by love	2:19; cf. 2:4	8:42; 13:34–35; 14:15–24; 15:9–17
Sheep and lambs	7:17; 14:4	10:1–16, 27–28; 21:15–17
Bride of Messiah	19:7; 21:2, 9; 22:17	3:29

Eschatology		
Present eschatology	1:6; 5:5; 12:9–11; 15:2	3:18; 5:24–25; 6:47; 12:31; 16:11, 33
Future eschatology	2:7, 17, 26–28; 3:5, 12, 21; 19:1–22:6	5:28–29; 6:40b; 14:2–4, 28–29; 18:36
Imagery		
Unnumbered sevens	Beatitudes (1:3 et al.); doxological language (5:12; 7:12)	Signs (2:11 et al.), "I am" sayings (6:35 et al.), disciples (21:2)
Manna/living bread	2:17	6:31–35, 48–58
God/Jesus as truth	3:7, 14; 6:10; 19:11	1:14, 17; 14:6; 15:26; 16:13
Door	3:8, 20	10:7, 9
Living water	7:16–17; 21:6; 22:1–2	4:10–15; 7:37–38
Child-bearing	12:2–5	16:21
Wine	14:8, 10; 16:19; 17:2; 18:3	2:3–10
Vine	14:18–19	15:1–5
Bride and groom	18:23; 19:7; 21:2, 9; 22:17	2:9; 3:29
God/Jesus as light	21:23–24; 22:5	1:4–9; 3:19–21; 8:12; 9:5; 12:35–36, 46

16. Thematic Parallels Among Revelation, Jude, and 2 Peter

Parallels	Revelation	Jude	2 Peter
Word(s) of prophecy mentioned	1:3; 19:10; 22:7, 10, 18, 19		1:19–21
Heretical teachers claim to be shepherds and apostles of Christ's flock	2:2	11–12	
Believers contend for the faith	2:13	3	1:5
False teachers accused of error of Balaam	2:14	11	2:15; 3:17
Believers lured into immorality	2:14, 20	4	2:14, 18
True and false knowledge contrasted	2:17, 24	10	1:2–3, 16
Believers exposed to false teaching	2:24	4	2:1
Christ likened to the morning star	2:28; 22:16		1:19
Appeal to remember teaching of true apostles	3:3	17	1:12; 3:1–2
Day of Christ likened to the thief	3:3; 16:15		3:10
Believers lured into contaminating their clothing	3:4—neg.	23	
Lord attended by myriads of angels	5:11	14	
Existing heavens and earth to disappear	6:14; 16:20; 20:11		3:10
God speaks through his prophets	10:7	14	1:19–21; 3:2
Sodom mentioned negatively	11:8	7	2:6
Egypt mentioned negatively	11:8	5	
Devil a disputer and deceiver	12:9; 20:2–3, 10	9	
Day of judgment to come	14:7	6	2:4, 9; 3:7
Fire the element of judgment	18:8; 20:9, 14, 15	7, 23	3:7, 10, 12
Fallen angels chained in depths of hell	20:1–3	6	2:4
Appeal made to theme of a thousand years	20:2–7		3:8
Heavens and earth to be replaced by the new	21:1		3:13
Apostles are foundation of church	21:14	17	
Book closes with "Amen"	22:21 (var.)	25	3:18

17. Thematic Parallels Between Revelation and 4 Ezra

Parallels	Revelation	4 Ezra
Province of Asia named	1:4	15:45; 16:1
Messiah coming on the clouds	1:7	13:3
Command to write down the vision	1:11	12:37
Sound of many waters	1:15	6:17
Touch by a heavenly being	1:17	5:15; 10:30
Tree of life in paradise	2:7; 22:2	2:12; 8:52
Faithful receive crowns from Son of God	2:10; 3:11	2:46–47
Worthy dressed in white clothing	3:4–5, 18; 6:11; 7:9, 13–14; 19:14	2:40
Earth's inhabitants portrayed negatively	3:10; 6:10; 8:13; 11:10; 13:8, 12, 14; 17:2, 8	3:9, 25, 34, 35; 6:18, 26; 11:32, 34; 12:24; 14:17, 20; 15:40
Heavenly city	3:12; 21:2–27	8:52; 10:42, 44
Lion as a messianic symbol	5:5	12:31–32
Saints cry, "How long?"	6:10	4:33, 35
Complete number of martyrs awaited	6:11	4:36
Four winds	7:1	13:5
A number of saints sealed	7:4	2:38
Tribes of Israel as symbol of God's people	7:4–8	13:39–40
Great multitude holding palm branches	7:9	2:42–46
Heavenly interpreter asked, "Who are these?"	7:13	2:44
Woes pronounced	8:13; 12:12; 18:10, 16, 19	2:8; 13:16, 19; 15:14, 24, 47; 16:1, 63, 77
Furnace located in the Abyss/pit	9:2	7:36
Multitude singing on Mount Zion	14:1	2:42
Babylon destroyed	14:8; 16; 18:2, 10, 21	15:43, 60
Babylon as a cipher for Rome	14:8; 16:19; 17:5; 18:2, 10, 21	15:43, 46, 60; 16:1
Metaphor of harvest as judgment	14:15	4:28, 35
Blood flowing as high as a horse	14:20	15:35
Falls down before an angel	19:10; 22:8–9	5:14; 10:30
Messiah's mouth acts as a weapon	19:15	13:10
War between Messiah and his enemies	19:19–20; 20:8–9	13:5, 8
Lake of fire	19:20; 20:10, 14, 15	7:36
Sea/earth give up dead for resurrection	20:13	7:32
Jerusalem as a glorious woman	21:2–10	10:25–27
Heavenly Jerusalem with large foundations	21:14–20	10:27
Kings of nations bring their splendor to God	21:24–26	15:20
Command to make public the book(s)	22:10	15:45
Messiah as offspring of David	22:16	12:32

18. Theme of Victory in Revelation[1]

A	B	C	D	E	D'	C'	B'	A'
				12:1–17				
		8:2–11:19		Present 12:11	13:1–16:21			
		3:21–8:5	Present 11:3–6		Present (Beast) 13:7	16:18–19:10		
	1:4–4:2	Past (Lamb) 5:5–6	Present (Beast) 11:7		Present 13:9–10, 18; 14:1–5, 12–13; 16:15	Future 19:1–2, 6–8	19:6–22:9	
1:1–8	Past (Lamb) 1:18; 3:21	Present (Beast) 6:2	Future 11:11–12, 18		Present (Lamb) 14:1, 4	Present 19:9	Future 20:4–6; 21:2–4	22:6–21
Present 1:3	Present 2:2–3, 9–10, 13, 19, 24–25; 3:4, 8–10	Future 6:9–11; 7:9–10, 13–17			Future 15:2–4	Future (Lamb) 19:11–16	Present 21:6–7	Future (Lamb) 22:7a, 12, 20
Past (Lamb) 1:5	Future 2:7, 10–11, 17, 26–28; 3:5, 12, 21							Present 22:7b
Future (Lamb) 1:7								Future 22:14, 17

1. See chiastic structure in chart 10.

19. Theories of Interpretation of Revelation

Historicist	Preterist	Futurist	Idealist	Eclectic
Major movements of Christian history predicted	Present situation only addressed, not a future period	Visions of 4:1–22:5 deal with a future time before the end of history	Symbolic portrayal of cosmic conflict between good and evil	Modified idealist perspective
Seven letters prophesy seven periods of church age	Book dated before A.D. 70 so a prophecy of Jerusalem's fall; Armageddon is siege of Jerusalem	Symbols to be interpreted literally	Universal depiction of struggle between God and Satan	Final coming of Christ to deliver, judge, and establish eternal kingdom is the only specific prophesied historical event
Historical events linked solely to Western church history	Jewish persecutors of church judged for apostasy	Ethnic Israel to be restored to its land	Symbols not related to historical events but portray timeless truths	Events throughout history portrayed symbolically
Antichrist often interpreted as the pope	Readers are assured they are the true Israel	Church raptured to heaven before seven-year Tribulation	Seal, trumpet, and bowl cycles show God's judgment on unbelievers at all times	Majority of events are transtemporal and applicable throughout church age
	Prophecy also about Roman persecution and fall of Roman Empire	Antichrist reigns on earth during Tribulation	1,000 years not future but contemporaneous with church age	Beast is many antichrists throughout church history as well as final Antichrist
		Evil nations gather to fight over Jerusalem but Christ defeats them at his second coming		
		Literal reign on earth of 1,000 years after which Satan rebels and is defeated in last battle		
		Following last judgment, Christ reigns eternally with saints in new heaven and new earth		

20. Five Senses in Revelation

Sight		
	Golden	1:13; 15:6
	White	1:14; 2:17; 3:4, 5, 18; 4:4; 6:2, 11; 7:9, 13, 14; 14:14; 19:11, 14; 20:11
	Rainbow	4:3; 10:1
	Red	6:4; 12:3
	Black	6:5, 12
	Green	6:8; 8:7; 9:4
	Blue	9:17
	Yellow	9:17
	Fiery	9:17; 10:1; 11:19
	Purple	17:4; 18:16; cf. 18:12
	Scarlet	17:4; 18:16; cf. 18:12
Taste		
	Lukewarm, hot, cold	3:16
	Bitter	8:11; 10:9, 10
	Sweet	10:9, 10
Smell		
	Incense	5:8; 8:3–5; cf. 18:13
	Cinnamon	cf. 18:13
	Myrrh	cf. 18:13
	Frankincense	cf. 18:13
Hearing		
	Voice	1:10, 12; 4:1; 5:2, 11, 12; 6:1, 6, 7; 7:2, 10; 8:13; 9:13; 10:4, 8; 11:12; 12:10; 14:2, 7, 9, 13, 15, 18; 16:1, 17; 18:2, 4; 19:1, 5, 6, 17; 21:3; cf. 18:23
	Rushing waters	cf. 1:15; 14:2; 19:6
	Thunder	4:5; 8:5; 11:19; 16:18; cf. 6:1; 14:2; 19:6
	Rumblings	4:5; 8:5; 11:19; 16:18
	Trumpets	8:7, 8, 10, 12; 9:1, 13; 11:15; 18:22
	Harps	14:2; 18:22
	Songs	18:22
	Flutes	18:22
	Millstones	18:22
Touch		
	Scroll	5:1; 10:2, 8, 10
	Harp, bowl	5:8
	Pair of scales	6:5
	Palm branches	7:9
	Reed	11:1
	Chain	20:1

21. Minerals, Gems, and Other Commodities in Revelation

Minerals		
	Gold	1:12, 20; 2:1; 3:18; 4:4; 5:8; 8:3; 9:7, 13, 20; 14:14; 15:7; 17:4; 18:12, 16; 21:15, 18, 21
	Bronze	1:15; 2:18; 9:20; 18:12
	Sulfur	9:17, 18; 14:10; 19:20; 20:10; 21:8
	Silver	9:20; 18:12
	Iron	18:12
Gems		
	Pearls	17:4; 18:12, 16; 21:21
	Jasper	4:3; 21:11, 18, 19
	Sapphire	21:19
	Agate/chalcedony	21:19
	Emerald	21:19
	Onyx/sardonyx	21:20
	Carnelian	4:3; 21:20
	Chrysolite	21:20
	Beryl	21:20
	Topaz	21:20
	Chrysoprase	21:20
	Jacinth	21:20
	Amethyst	21:20
Other Commodities		
	Stone	2:17; 9:20; 18:21
	Glass	4:6; 15:2; 21:18, 21
	Crystal	4:6; 22:1
	Wood	9:20; 18:12
	Citron	18:12
	Ivory	18:12
	Marble	18:12

22. Symbols Interpreted in Revelation

Text	Symbol	Interpretation
1:20	Seven stars	Angels of the seven churches
1:20	Seven lampstands	Seven churches
2:9; 3:9	Synagogue of Satan	Those who say they are Jews but are not
4:5	Seven blazing lamps	Seven spirits, or sevenfold Spirit, of God
5:8; 8:3–4	Golden bowls of incense	Prayers of the saints
7:9, 13–14	Great multitude	Those wearing white robes who have come out of the Great Tribulation
8:10–11	Great blazing star	Named Wormwood, meaning bitterness
9:11	Angel of the Abyss	Hebrew name is Abaddon, Greek name is Apollyon, both meaning Destroyer
11:3–4	Two witnesses	Two olive trees and two lampstands that stand before the Lord of the earth
11:8	Great city	Sodom and Egypt, where also the Lord was crucified
12:5	Male child	Son who will rule all nations with an iron scepter
12:9; 20:2	Great Dragon	Ancient Serpent, Devil, Satan
12:17	Offspring of the woman	Those who obey God's commandments and hold to the testimony of Jesus
13:18	666	Number of the Beast and a man's number
14:1, 3–4	144,000	Virgins redeemed from the earth who did not defile themselves with women
16:13–14	Three evil spirits	Demonic spirits that perform miraculous signs and gather the kings for battle
16:16	Harmagedon (Armageddon)	In Hebrew, place where kings are gathered for the great battle
17:1, 15	Many waters	Peoples, multitudes, nations, and languages
17:3, 5	Woman sitting on a scarlet beast	Mother of prostitutes and of the abominations of the earth
17:3, 5, 18	Woman sitting on a scarlet beast	Great city Babylon that rules over the kings of the earth
17:3, 7, 9	Seven heads of scarlet beast	Seven hills on which the woman sits
17:3, 7, 10	Seven heads of scarlet beast	Seven kings: five fallen, one is, one has not yet come
17:3, 7, 12	Ten horns of scarlet beast	Ten kings who have not yet received a kingdom but will rule for one hour
19:8	Bride's fine linen	Righteous acts of the saints
19:11, 16	Rider on a white horse	King of kings and Lord of lords
20:5	1,000 years	First resurrection
20:8	Gog and Magog	Nations in the four corners of the earth
20:14; 21:8	Lake of fire	Second death
21:2, 9–10	Holy City, New Jerusalem	Bride, the wife of the Lamb

23. Use of Numbers in Revelation

1/10	A tenth of the city (11:13)
1/4	A fourth of the earth (6:8)
1/3	A third of the earth (8:7)
	A third of the trees (8:7)
	A third of the sea (8:8)
	A third of the living creatures (8:9)
	A third of the ships (8:9)
	A third of the rivers (8:10)
	A third of the waters (8:11)
	A third of the sun (8:12)
	A third of the moon (8:12)
	A third of the stars (8:12; 12:4)
	A third of humanity (9:15, 18)
1/2	A half hour (8:1)
1	One hour (17:12; 18:10, 17, 19)
	One purpose (17:13)
	One day (18:8)
2	Two witnesses (11:3)
	Two olive trees (11:4)
	Two lampstands (11:4)
	Two prophets (11:10)
	Two wings (12:14)
	Two horns (13:11)
	Two beasts (19:20)
3	Three quarts (6:6)
	Three angels (8:13)
	Three plagues (9:18)
	Three unclean spirits (16:13)
	Three parts (16:19)
	Three gates (21:13)
3½	Three and a half days (11:9, 11)
	Three and a half times (12:14)
4	Four living creatures (4:6, 8; 5:6, 8, 14; 6:1, 6; 7:11; 14:3; 15:7; 19:4)
	Four angels (7:1, 2; 9:14, 15)
	Four corners (7:1; 20:8)
	Four winds (7:1)
5	Five months (9:5, 10)
6	Six wings (4:8)
7	Seven churches (1:4, 11, 20)

	Seven spirits (1:4; 3:1; 4:5; 5:6)	
	Seven lampstands (1:12, 20; 2:1)	
	Seven stars (1:16, 20; 2:1; 3:1)	
	Seven lamps (4:5)	
	Seven seals (5:1, 5; 6:1)	
	Seven horns (5:6)	
	Seven eyes (5:6)	
	Seven angels (8:2, 6; 15:1, 6, 7, 8; 16:1; 17:1; 21:9)	
	Seven trumpets (8:2, 6)	
	Seven thunders (10:3, 4)	
	Seven heads (12:3; 13:1; 17:3, 7, 9)	
	Seven crowns (12:3)	
	Seven plagues (15:1, 6, 8; 21:9)	
	Seven bowls (15:7; 16:1; 17:1; 21:9)	
	Seven hills (17:9)	
	Seven kings (17:10)	
10	Ten days (2:10)	
	Ten horns (12:3; 13:1; 17:3, 7, 12, 16)	
	Ten diadems (13:1)	
	Ten kings (17:12)	
12	Twelve stars (12:1)	
	Twelve gates (21:12, 21)	
	Twelve angels (21:12)	
	Twelve tribes (21:12)	
	Twelve foundations (21:14)	
	Twelve names (21:14)	
	Twelve apostles (21:14)	
	Twelve pearls (21:21)	
	Twelve fruits (22:2)	
24	Twenty-four thrones (4:4)	
	Twenty-four elders (4:4, 10; 5:8; 11:16; 19:4)	
42	Forty-two months (11:2; 13:5)	
144	One hundred forty-four cubits (21:17)	
666	Six hundred sixty-six: number of man (13:18)	
1,000	One thousand years (20:2, 3, 4, 5, 6, 7)	
1,260	One thousand two hundred sixty days (11:3; 12:6)	
7,000	Seven thousand people (11:13)	
12,000	Twelve thousand of each tribe sealed (7:5, 6, 7, 8)	
	Twelve thousand stadia (21:16)	
144,000	One hundred forty-four thousand servants (7:4; 14:1, 3)	
200,000,000	Two hundred million troops (9:16)	

24. Symbolism of Colors and Numbers in Revelation

Colors	Reference(s)	Symbolism
Golden	1:13; 15:6	Divinity, splendor
White	1:14; 2:17; 3:4, 5, 18; 4:4; 6:2, 11; 7:9, 13, 14; 14:14; 19:11, 14; 20:11	Victory, purity, resurrection
Rainbow	4:3; 10:1	Omnipotence
Red	6:4; 12:3	Slaughter, war, violence
Black	6:5, 12	Disaster, famine
Green	6:8; 8:7; 9:4	Death
Blue	9:17	Smoke
Yellow	9:17	Sulfur
Fiery	9:17; 10:1; 11:19	Judgment
Purple	17:4; 18:16; cf. 18:12	Royalty
Scarlet	17:4; 18:16; cf. 18:12	Royalty
Numbers		
1/2	8:1	Short, brief
1	17:12; 18:8, 10, 17, 19	Exclusiveness, primacy, excellence
2	11:3, 4, 10; 12:14; 13:11; 19:20	Plurality
3	6:6; 8:13; 9:18;16:13, 19, 21:13	Sufficiency; limited plurality
3½	11:9, 11; 12:14	Final period of Satan's rule
4	4:6, 8; 5:6, 8, 14; 6:1, 6; 7:1, 2; 9:10, 14, 15; 14:3; 15:7; 19:4; 20:8	Cosmic completeness
5	9:5, 10	Limited
6	4:8	Incompletion
7	1:4, 11, 12, 16, 20; 2:1; 3:1; 4:5; 5:1, 5, 6; 6:1; 8:2, 6; 10:3, 4; 12:3; 13:1; 15:1, 6, 7, 8; 16:1; 17:1, 3, 7, 9, 10, 11; 21:9	Perfection, completeness
10	2:10; 12:3; 13:1; 17:3, 7, 12, 16	Fullness, completeness
12	12:1; 21:12, 14, 21; 22:2	Completeness; number of God's people
24	4:4, 10; 5:8; 11:16; 19:4	12 x 2
42	11:2; 13:5	42 ÷ 12 = 3½
144	21:17	12 x 12
666	13:18	Man's number
1,000	20:2, 3, 4, 5, 6, 7	Enumeration of large numbers
1,260	11:3; 12:6	1,260 ÷ 30 = 42
7,000	11:13	7 x 1,000
12,000	7:5, 6, 7, 8; 21:16	12 x 1,000
144,000	7:4; 14:1, 3	12 x 12 x 1,000

25. Figures of Speech in Revelation

Reference	Simile
1:10	Loud voice like (ὡς) a trumpet
1:13	Someone like (ὅμοιον) a Son of Man
1:14	Head and hair white like wool, as white as snow; eyes like blazing fire
1:15	Feet like burnished bronze, as glowing in a furnace; his voice like the sound of rushing waters
1:16	Face like the sun shining in all its brilliance
1:17	I fell as though dead
2:18	Eyes like blazing fire; feet like burnished bronze
2:27	Break them like clay pots
3:3	Come like a thief
4:1	Voice speaking like a trumpet
4:3	Someone whose appearance is like jasper and carnelian, rainbow whose appearance is like an emerald
4:6	Something like a sea of glass, like crystal
4:7	First living creature like a lion, the second like an ox, the third with a face like a man, the fourth like a flying eagle
5:6	Lamb standing as slain
6:1	Voice like thunder
6:6	Something like a voice
6:12	Sun black as goat-hair sackcloth; moon (red) as blood
6:13	Stars of heaven fell as a fig tree drops its late figs
6:14	Heaven receded like a scroll rolling up
8:8	Something like a large mountain
8:10	Great star burning like a torch
9:2	Smoke rose like smoke from a large furnace
9:5	Torment like a scorpion's sting
9:7	Locusts' appearance like horses prepared for battle; something like crowns of gold; faces like human faces
9:8	Hair like woman's hair; teeth like lion's teeth
9:9	Breastplates like breastplates of iron; wings sound like many horse-drawn chariots charging into battle
9:10	Tails with stingers like scorpions
9:17	Horses' heads like heads of lions
9:19	Tails like snakes
10:1	Face like the sun; legs like fiery pillars
10:9, 10	Scroll sweet as honey
11:1	Reed like a measuring rod
12:15	Water like a river
13:2	Beast like a leopard, feet like a bear's, mouth like a lion's
14:2	Sound like that of many waters, like that of great thunder, like harpists playing their harps

14:14	Someone like a Son of Man
15:2	Something like a sea of glass mixed with fire
16:3	Blood like that of a corpse
16:13	Three unclean spirits like frogs
16:15	Come like a thief
18:21	Boulder like a large millstone
19:1, 6	Sound like that of a great multitude
19:6	Sound like that of many waters, like that of great thunder
19:12	Eyes like a flame of fire
20:8	Number like the sand of the sea
21:11	City's brilliance like a very precious stone, like a crystal-clear jasper
21:18	Pure gold like clear glass
21:21	Street like transparent glass
22:1	River clear as crystal
Metaphor	
1:1; 2:20; 7:3; 10:7; 11:18; 15:3; 19:2, 5; 22:3, 6	Servant, slave
1:5	To free from sin
1:6; 5:10; 20:6	Priest
1:16	Seven stars
1:16; 2:12, 16; 19:15, 21	Sharp double-edged sword out of the mouth
1:18; 9:1; 20:1	Key(s)
2:7, 11, 17, 26; 3:5, 12, 21; 5:5; 12:11; 17:14; 21:7	Be victorious/conquer/triumph
2:7; 22:2, 14, 19	Tree of life
2:10	Wreath/crown of life
2:11; 20:6, 14; 21:8	Second death
2:13	Throne of Satan
2:17	Hidden manna; white stone
2:20	Jezebel
2:27; 19:15	Iron scepter
2:28; 22:16	Morning star
3:2; 16:15	Be watchful/wake up
3:4, 18; 16:15	Clothes
3:4–5; 4:4; 19:14	Dressed in white
3:5	Erase/blot out
3:5; 13:8; 17:8; 20:12, 15; 21:27	Book of Life
3:7	Key of David

3:8	Open door
3:11	Take away your wreath/crown
3:12	Pillar; write God's name and name of God's city on him; new name
3:12; 11:1; 21:22	Temple
3:12; 21:2	New Jerusalem
3:15–16	Hot; cold
3:16	Spit/vomit
3:18; 16:15	Shameful nakedness
3:20	Christ knocking at the door; eating together
3:21	Sit with me on my throne
5:1	Right hand
5:5	Lion of the tribe of Judah
5:5; 22:16	Root (and offspring) of David
5:6 (+28 more)	Lamb
5:8; 8:3, 4	Incense
5:8; 14:2; 15:2	Harp
6:4	Large sword
6:11; 7:9, 13, 14	White robe
6:13	Stars fell
7:4; 14:1, 3	144,000
7:14	Washed their robes
7:17	Shepherd
8:3	Incense offering
10:9, 10	Eating the scroll
10:10	Turned sour/became bitter
11:1, 2; 21:15	Measuring rod
11:2, 3; 12:6, 14	42 months/1,260 days/time, times, and half a time
11:4	Two olive trees; two lampstands
11:5	Fire from their mouths
11:8	Sodom; Egypt
11:8; 16:19; 17:18; 18:10, 16, 18, 19, 21	Great city
11:18; 22:12	Reward
12:1, 6, 13–17	The woman
12:2	Woman bearing a child
12:3; 13:1; 17:3, 7, 9	Seven heads, ten horns
12:15	Sweep away
13:3	Whole earth
13:6	To blaspheme God's dwelling place
14:4	Virgins; to redeem; firstfruits
14:8; 16:19; 17:5; 18:2, 10, 21	Babylon

14:10; 17:4; 18:6	Cup
14:11, 13	Rest
14:15–16	Grain harvest
14:17–20	Grape harvest
14:19, 20; 19:15	Winepress
17:1, 15, 16; 19:2	Great prostitute
17:1, 15	Many waters
17:2	Sexual immorality, intoxication
17:4	Golden cup
17:6	Drunk with the blood
17:9	Seven hills
17:16	Leave her naked; eat her flesh; burn her with fire
18:5	Piled up to heaven
18:7	Widow
18:14	Fruit
19:7; 21:9	Wife
19:9	Wedding feast
19:11	White horse
19:12	Many crowns
19:20; 20:10, 14, 15	Lake of fire burning with sulfur
20:2	To bind
20:2, 3, 4, 5, 6, 7	1,000 years
20:8	Gog and Magog
20:9	Camp of God's people
20:11	Great White Throne
20:12	Books
21:2, 9; 22:17	Bride
21:7	My son
21:27; 22:14	Entering the city
22:4	His face
22:17	Thirsty for water
	Personification
1:12; 4:1	"The voice" for voice of God
1:18; 6:8; 20:13, 14	"Death" refers to a person; "Hades" to his kingdom
5:13	Every creature singing
9:1–2	"Star" for doorkeeper
9:3–6	"Locusts" for army
9:11	"Abaddon" and "Apollyon" for angel over place of dead
9:13	Horns of altar speaking
12:3–6	"Dragon" for Satan
12:15	Serpent spewed water

12:16	Earth opened mouth and swallowed
13:1	"Beast out of the sea" for Roman emperor and his proconsul
13:11	"Beast out of the earth" for Asiarch who was priest of imperial cult
16:7	"Altar" for martyred saints and prophets
17:3–18	"The woman" (Roma) for Rome
17:12	"Ten horns" for ten kings
21:2	"Holy city, new Jerusalem" for an adorned bride
22:15	"Dogs" for sodomite
22:17	"Bride" for the church
Apostrophe	
18:10, 16, 19	"Woe! Woe, O great city . . ."
18:23	"Your merchants . . . your sorcery"
Parody	
2:24	"Deep things of Satan" perhaps a parody of motto "deep things of Jezebel"
6:8	To kill with a sword parodies Roman *ius gladii* (the right of execution)
13:1	Beast's appearance parodies Christ
13:1	Ten horns suggest universal rule parodying Christ's sovereign rule
13:3	Beast's fatal wound and healing parodies death and resurrection of Lamb (cf. 5:6)
13:4	"Who is like . . . ?" parodies similar OT questions used in OT hymns
13:11	Beast with two horns parodies appearance of Lamb
13:16	Mark of Beast parodies seal of the living God (cf. 7:3; 9:4)
17:8, 11	Beast who was, is not, and is to come parodies God who was, and is, and is to come (4:8; cf. 1:4, 8)
19:17	Great supper of God parodies the wedding supper of the Lamb
Metonymy	
2:3	"My name" refers to person of exalted Christ
6:6	"Oil and wine" refers to olive trees and grapevines
7:9	"Palm branches" refer to victory
7:14	"Blood of the Lamb" refers to atoning death of Christ
11:18	"The earth" refers to the people of the earth
Merism	
1:8; 21:6; 22:13	Alpha and Omega
1:17; 2:8; 22:13	First and last
21:6; 22:13	Beginning and end
Euphemism	
6:11	Rest/wait
17:10; cf. 14:8; 18:2	Fallen

	Paradox
2:9; 3:9	Synagogue of Satan
3:1	Reputation of being alive but are dead
3:16	Neither hot nor cold but lukewarm
3:17	Claim to be rich but wretched and poor
	Hyperbole
4:8; 7:15	Day and night
7:9	Great multitude that no one could count
9:16	Two hundred million
14:20	Blood to the height of the horses' bridles
18:5	Sins piled up to heaven
19:3	Her smoke rises forever and ever
	Irony
3:9	Jews to fall down at the feet of Gentile believers
3:17	Laodiceans poor, blind, and naked
5:5–6	Lion becomes Lamb

26. Doublets in Revelation

Doublets	First Image	Second Image
Two thrones	Throne of God (40x)	Throne of Satan (2:13; 13:2)
Two riders on white horses	Conqueror with bow and crown (6:2)	Conqueror with sword and scepter (19:11, 15)
Two marks	Seal of God (7:3–4; 9:4)	Mark of Beast (13:17; 14:9, 11; 16:2; 19:20; 20:4)
Two multitudes	144,000 from Israel's twelve tribes (7:4–8; 14:1–5)	Great multitude from every nation, tribe, people, and language (7:9–14; 19:1, 6)
Two witnesses	Two olive trees (11:4)	Two lampstands (11:4)
Two beasts	Beast out of sea (13:1–8)	Beast out of land (13:11–17)
Two harvests	Grain (14:15–16)	Grapes (14:18–19)
Two cities	New Jerusalem (3:12; 21:2, 10)	Babylon the Great (14:8; 16:19; 17:5; 18:2, 10, 21)
Two women	Great Prostitute (17:1–18; 19:2)	Bride of Lamb (19:7; 21:2, 9)
Two banquets	Wedding supper of Lamb (19:7)	Great supper of God (19:17)
Two angels worshiped	John falls down (19:10)	John falls down (22:8)
Two battles	Armies of the Beast, False Prophet, and kings defeated (19:19–21)	Nations of Satan defeated (20:7–9)
Two heavens	First heaven (21:1)	New heaven (21:1)
Two earths	First earth (21:1)	New earth (21:1)

27. Paired Characters in Revelation

Lamb (Christ)	Beast
Shares power, authority, and throne of God (3:21; 5:6; 7:17; 12:10; 22:1, 3)	Shares power, authority, and throne of Dragon (13:2, 7; 16:10; 17:13)
Triumphed over enemies (5:5)	Triumphs over the saints (11:7; 13:7)
Slaughtered but living (5:6)	Wounded fatally but healed (13:3, 12)
Rules over every tribe, language, people, and nation (5:9; 7:9)	Rules over every tribe, people, language, and nation (13:7; cf. 11:9)
Every creature worships him (5:13)	Earth dwellers worship the Beast (13:4, 8, 12, 15; 14:11; 16:2; 19:20)
Seal/mark on forehead of followers (7:3; 9:4; 14:1; cf. 22:4)	Mark on forehead of followers (13:16; 14:9; 20:4)
Has names—Faithful and True, Word of God and King of kings and Lord of lords (19:11, 13, 16)	Has blasphemous names (13:1; 17:3)
Wears many diadems (19:12)	Wears ten diadems (13:1)

Two Witnesses	Beast out of the Earth
Receive (authority?) from Lamb (11:3)	Receives authority from first beast (13:12)
Prophets who prophesy (11:3, 6, 10)	False Prophet (16:13; 19:20; 20:10)
Two olive trees; two lampstands (11:4)	Two horns (13:11)
Fire comes from their mouths (11:5)	Causes fire to come from heaven (13:13)
Perform great signs (11:6)	Performs great signs (13:13, 14; 19:20)
Torment earth dwellers (11:10)	Deceives earth dwellers (13:14; 19:20)
Receive breath of life from God (11:11)	Gives breath to image of first beast (13:15)
Taken up to heaven (11:12)	Cast into lake of fire (19:20; 20:10)

Bride	Prostitute
Wife of the Lamb (19:7; 21:9)	Mother of prostitutes (17:5)
Dressed in fine linen, bright and clean (19:8; 21:2)	Dressed in purple and scarlet (17:4)
Related to Holy City (21:2)	Related to great city Babylon (17:5, 18)
Sits on a high mountain (21:10)	Sits on seven hills (17:9)
Adorned with gold and precious jewels (21:11, 18–21)	Adorned with gold, precious stones, and pearls (17:4; 18:16)
Everything unclean banned (21:27)	Haunt of every unclean thing (18:2)
Drinks of river of water of life (22:1)	Drinks of cup of abominations (17:4)
Seen by John in new heaven and earth (21:2, 10)	Seen by John in desert (17:3)

28. Angels and Demons in Revelation

Reference	Description	Activity
Angels		
1:1	His angel	Shows revelation to John
1:16, 20	Seven stars held by Jesus	Interpreted as angels of the seven churches
2:1, 8, 12, 18; 3:1, 7, 14	Angel of the church	Receive letters to Ephesus, Smyrna, Pergamum, Thyatira, Sardis, Philadelphia, Laodicea
3:5	His angels	Victors' names to be acknowledged by Jesus before the angels
5:2	Mighty angel	Asks loudly who is worthy to open the scroll
5:11	Myriads of angels around the throne	Declare loudly, "Worthy is the Lamb"
7:1–2	Four angels standing at the four corners of the earth	Hold back the four winds preventing any wind from blowing on the earth
7:2–3	Angel from the east	Calls out to four angels not to harm the land or sea until God's servants are sealed
7:11	Angels standing around the throne	Fall on their faces and worship God
8:2, 6, 7, 8, 10, 12; 9:1, 13; 11:15	Seven angels given seven trumpets by God	Angels sound trumpets, thereby releasing judgments upon the earth
8:3–5	Angel with a golden censer	Offers incense at the heavenly altar before hurling the censer to the earth
9:14	Sixth angel	Announces the release of the four angels
9:15	Four angels bound at the Euphrates River	Kill a third of the earth's inhabitants
10:1–11	Mighty angel coming down from heaven	Swears that the mystery of God will be accomplished without delay, then gives John the little scroll to eat
12:7	Michael and his angels	Fight the Dragon and his angels
14:6	Angel flying in midair	Proclaims the eternal gospel to those living on earth
14:8	Second angel flying in midair	Declares that Babylon the Great is fallen
14:9–11	Third angel flying in midair	Announces loudly that anyone who receives the Beast's mark will be tormented in the presence of the holy angels and the Lamb
14:15	Angel coming out of the temple	Calls loudly to someone sitting on a cloud to begin the earth's harvest
14:17–19	Another angel coming out of the temple in heaven	Holds a sharp sickle and harvests the grapes, then throws them into the winepress of God's wrath
14:18	Another angel in charge of the fire comes from the altar	Loudly directs the angel with the sickle to begin the grape harvest
15:1, 6–8	Seven angels dressed in clean, shining linen and wearing golden sashes around their chests	Receive the seven last plagues from one of the four living creatures
16:1, 2, 3, 4, 8, 10, 12, 17	Seven angels with seven bowls	Voice from the temple tells them to pour out the seven bowls of God's wrath on the earth
16:5	Angel in charge of the waters	Declares that God's judgments are just

17:1–3, 7, 15	One of seven angels with the bowls	Shows John the great prostitute by carrying him to the wilderness, then explains the mystery of the woman and of the beast she rides
18:1–3	Angel with great authority and splendor coming from heaven	Shouts in a loud voice that Babylon the Great has fallen
18:21–24	Mighty angel	Throws large boulder into the sea and declares that normal life in Babylon the Great is over
19:9–10	Inferred angel who is John's fellow servant	Directs John to write a beatitude but refuses worship when John falls at his feet
19:17–18	Angel standing in the sun	Cries loudly to the birds and invites them to the great supper of God
20:1–3	Angel coming from heaven, holding the key to the Abyss and a great chain	Seizes the Dragon and binds him in the Abyss for a thousand years
21:9, 15–21	One of seven angels with the bowls who has a golden measuring rod	Carries John in the Spirit to see the Lamb's bride—the Holy City, Jerusalem—then measures the city, its gates, and walls
21:12	Twelve angels	At the twelve gates of the heavenly city
22:1–6, 8–11	Angel with measuring rod who declares that he is John's fellow servant	Shows John the heavenly city, declares the trustworthiness of his words, refuses John's worship, and directs him not to seal up the prophecy
22:16	My angel	Sent by Jesus to give John this testimony (cf. 1:1)
Demons		
9:3–11	Locusts (?)	Rise out of the Abyss and torture the earth's inhabitants for five months
9:11	Angel of the Abyss	King over the locusts, whose name in Hebrew is Abaddon and in Greek is Apollyon, meaning Destroyer
9:20	Demons	Worshiped by those not killed by the plagues
12:7–9	Dragon's angels	Defeated by Michael and his angels and cast down to earth
16:13–14	Evil spirits or spirits of demons appearing as frogs	Come out of the mouths of the Dragon, Beast, and False Prophet, and by performing signs gather the kings to the battle of Harmagedon
18:2	Demons and every evil spirit	Dwell now in fallen Babylon

29. Seven Beatitudes and Their Relationship to the Coming/Victor Sayings

Seven Beatitudes	Seven Coming/Victor Sayings	Church
1. Blessed are those who hear the words of the prophecy and keep them (1:3)	You have heard, now keep and repent (3:3)	Sardis
2. Blessed are the dead who die in the Lord from now on (14:13)	Become faithful until death (2:10)	Smyrna
3. Blessed are those watching for his coming as a thief (16:15)	Become watchful or Christ will come as a thief (3:2–3)	Sardis
4. Blessed are those invited to the marriage dinner of the Lamb (19:9)	Christ will dine with him (3:20)	Laodicea
5. Blessed are those in first resurrection because second death has no authority over them (20:6)	Second death will not harm victors (2:11)	Smyrna
6. Blessed are those keeping the words of the prophecy (22:7; cf. 22:9)	You have kept my word (3:10; cf. 3:8)	Philadelphia
7. Blessed are those washing their robes for they have the right to the tree of life (22:14)	Victor to eat from the tree of life (2:7)	Ephesus

30. Epithets of Jesus with Old and New Testament Background

Opening Vision	Seven Letters	Later Visions	OT and NT Background
Has seven stars in right hand (1:16)	Holds seven stars in right hand (2:1); has the seven stars (3:1)		
Among seven golden lampstands (1:12–13)	Walks among seven golden lampstands (2:1)		Golden lampstand with seven lights (Zech. 4:2)
First and Last (1:17)	First and Last (2:8)	First and Last (22:13)	First and last (Isa. 41:4; 44:6; 48:12)
Living One who died and lives again forever (1:18)	Died and lived again (2:8)		One who lives forever (Deut. 32:40; Dan. 4:34; 12:7)
Sharp double-edged sword out of his mouth (1:16)	Has sharp double-edged sword (2:12); sword of his mouth (2:16)	Sharp sword out of his mouth (19:15)	Mouth like a sharpened sword (Isa. 49:2); cf. rod of his mouth (Isa. 11:4)
Son of Man (1:13)	Son of God (2:18)	Son of Man (14:14)	My son (Ps. 2:7); Son of Man (Dan. 7:13)
Eyes like flame of fire (1:14)	Eyes like flame of fire (2:18)	Eyes like flame of fire (19:12)	Eyes like torches of fire (Dan. 10:6)
Feet like burnished bronze (1:15)	Feet like burnished bronze (2:18)		Legs like polished bronze (Dan. 10:6)
Ruler of kings of the earth (1:5)	Received Father's authority (2:27)	Rules nations with iron scepter (12:5; 19:15)	Son to rule nations with an iron scepter (Ps. 2:9)
Sevenfold Spirit (1:4)	Has sevenfold Spirit of God (3:1)	Sevenfold Spirit (4:5; 5:6)	Sevenfold Spirit (cf. Isa. 11:2–3 LXX)
	Holy (3:7)	Holy (cf. 6:10)	Holy One (Ps. 16:10; Isa. 1:4; 37:23; Hab. 3:3)
	True (3:7); true witness (3:14)	True (cf. 6:10); True (19:11)	True God (Isa. 65:16 LXX)
Has keys of death and Hades (1:18)	Has key of David to open and close (3:7)	Opens scroll and its seven seals (5:5, 9; 6:1ff.); star and angel given key to open Abyss (9:1; 20:1)	Holds the key to the house of David (Isa. 22:22); has keys of the kingdom of heaven (Matt. 16:19)
Amen (cf. 1:6, 7)	Amen (3:14)	Amen (cf. 22:20)	God of amen (Isa. 65:16 MT)
Faithful witness (1:5)	Faithful witness (3:14)	Faithful (19:11)	Faithful witness (Ps. 89:37)
Firstborn of the dead (1:5)	Beginning of God's creation (3:14)	Beginning and end (22:13)	Firstborn of all creation; the beginning, the firstborn from the dead (Col. 1:15, 18)

31. Suggested Divisions of the Letters in Revelation 2–3

Aune	Boring	Hubert	Roberts	Hahn
Adscriptio	Address to the angel	The address	Instruction to write	The messenger formula
Command to write	The city	The title of Christ	Announcement of sender	ὁιδα-section
τάδε λέγει formula	Prophetic messenger formula	The positive report	Diagnosis of the situation	The roll call
Christological predications	Christological ascription	The negative report	Call to conversion (not to Thyatira)	The overcomer saying
Narratio begun by οἶδα-clause	The divine knowledge	The exhortations	Threats, rewards, encouragements, counsel	
Dispositio	The "body"	The threats	Warning to listen	
Proclamation formula	The call to attention and obedience	The reward	Promise to those who triumph	
Promise of victory	Eschatological promise to the victors			

32. Structure of the Seven Letters in Revelation 2–3

Address Saying	Command to write to the angel of each church
Epithet Saying	Descriptive title of Jesus drawn largely from the opening vision
Praise Saying	Commendation for each church's positive deeds
Blame Saying	Rebuke for each church's negative deeds
Coming Saying	Call to repent with imminent judgment for unrepentance or warning of coming persecution
Hearing Saying	Call to hear and obey what the Spirit is saying to the churches
Victor Saying	Eschatological promises given to the victors who overcome

	Ephesus	Smyrna	Pergamum	Thyatira	Sardis	Philadelphia	Laodicea
Address	2:1a	2:8a	2:12a	2:18a	3:1a	3:7a	3:14a
Epithet	2:1b	2:8b	2:12b	2:18b	3:1b	3:7b	3:14b
Praise	2:2–3, 6	2:9	2:13	2:19, 24a	3:4	3:8	
Blame	2:4		2:14–15	2:20–21	3:1c		3:15–17
Coming	2:5	2:10a	2:16	2:22–23, 24b–25	3:2–3	3:9–11	3:18–20
Hearing	2:7a	2:11a	2:17a	2:29	3:6	3:13	3:22
Victor	2:7b	2:10b, 11b	2:17b	2:26–28	3:5	3:12	3:21

33. An Imperial Edict Compared
to the Letter to Ephesus

Sections	Augustus's Decree to Ephesus	Letter to Ephesus (2:1–7)
Praescriptio	Caesar August, Pontifex Maximus with tribunician powers says (λέγει)	Thus says (Τάδε λέγει) him who holds the seven stars in his right hand
Prooemium	Absent	Absent
Promulgatio	Absent	Absent
Narratio	Since the Jewish nation has been found (εὑρέθη) well disposed to the Roman people not only at the present time but also in time past . . .	I know (οἶδα) your works—your toil and your endurance—and that you are not able to tolerate evil deeds . . .
Dispositio	it has been decided (ἔδοξέ) by me and my council under oath, with the consent of the Roman people. . . . And if anyone is caught stealing their sacred books or their sacred monies . . . he shall be regarded as sacrilegious and his property shall be confiscated to the public treasury. . . . I order (κελεύω) that it and the present edict be set up in the most conspicuous part of the temple constructed for me by the *koinon* of Asia in Pergamum.	Remember from where you have fallen; repent and do your first works. If you do not, I am coming to you and I will move your lampstand from its place, that is, if you do not repent.
Sanctio	If anyone transgresses any of the above ordinances, he shall suffer (δώσει) severe punishment	To the victor I will grant (δώσω) him to eat from the tree of life, which is in the paradise of God

34. Promise Images in the Seven Letters with Background in Jewish Literature

Images Texts	Tree	Paradise	Death	Crown	Stone	Name	Rod	Star	Garments
Revelation 2–3									
Ephesus	2:7	2:7							
Smyrna			2:10, 11	2:10					
Pergamum					2:17	2:17			
Thyatira			2:23				2:27	2:28	
Sardis						3:5			3:4–5
Philadelphia				3:11		3:12			
Laodicea									3:18
Old Testament									
Isaiah 61–62				61:3; 62:3		62:2			61:3, 10
Ezekiel 28 LXX		28:13		28:12	28:13				
Daniel 7									7:9
Zechariah 3				3:5	3:9				3:4, 5
Extrabiblical									
1 Enoch 90							90:18		90:31
4 Ezra 8	8:52	8:52	8:58–59						
Ascension of Isaiah 9				9:11–12, 18, 24–25					9:9, 11, 17–18, 24–26

35. Promises with Fulfillments and Relationship to Faithful Works

Church	Promises	Fulfillments	Faithful Works
Ephesus	Tree of life (2:7)	Tree of life (22:2, 14, 19)	Hate works of Nicolaitans (2:6)
	Paradise of God (2:7)	River of living water (22:1, 17)	
Smyrna	Crown of life (2:10)	First resurrection (20:5–6)	
	Deliverance from second death (2:11)	"Second" death (20:6, 14; 21:8)	Not to fear suffering and death (2:10)
Pergamum	Hidden manna (2:17)	Wedding supper (19:9)	To abstain from eating idol meat (2:14)
	White stone (2:17)	Precious stone (21:19)?	
	New name known only to recipient (2:17)	Name known only to himself (19:12)	Hold on to my name (2:13)
Thyatira	Authority over the nations (2:26)	Authority to judge (20:4)	Practice love, faith, service, and endurance (2:19)
	Rule with iron scepter (2:27)	Rule with iron scepter (19:15)	
	Morning Star (2:28)	Morning Star (22:16)	Ignorant of deep things of Satan (2:24)
Sardis	White garments (3:5)	White robes/linen (6:11; 7:9, 13; 19:8, 14; cf. 21:2; 22:14)	Keep garments white, not soiling them (3:4)
	Book of Life (3:5)	Book of Life (13:8; 20:12, 15; 21:27)	
	Confession of name (3:5)	(cf. Matt. 10:32; Luke 12:8)	To regain name for being alive (3:1)
Philadelphia	Pillar in the temple (3:12)	God and the Lamb are the temple (21:22)	Endure Jewish opposition (3:9–10)
	Names of God, God's city, and new name of Christ written (3:12)	Names of God and the Lamb written (14:1; 22:4)	Do not deny Christ's name (3:8)
	New Jerusalem descending from heaven (3:12)	New Jerusalem descending from heaven (21:2, 10)	
Laodicea	Sit on divine throne (3:21)	Martyrs seated on thrones (20:4)	To seek heavenly riches instead of worldly power and wealth (3:17–18)

36. Rhetorical Situation of the Church in Revelation

Seven Churches of Asia

Church	Threat	Persecutor	Spiritual Problem
Ephesus	Internal		Loss of first love; false apostles/Nicolaitans
Smyrna	External	Jews	None
Pergamum	External/Internal	Romans	Balaamites/Nicolaitans
Thyatira	Internal		Jezebelites
Sardis	Internal		Spiritually dead
Philadelphia	External	Jews	None
Laodicea	Internal		Spiritually lukewarm

Universal Church on Earth and in Heaven

Reference	Location	Description	Identification
6:9–11	Heaven (under altar)	Martyred souls crying for vengeance	Wearing white robes
7:1–8	Earth	144,000 from tribes of Israel	Seal on foreheads, called servants
7:9–14	Heaven (before throne)	Great multitude from every nation, tribe, people, and language worship and serve	Wearing white robes and holding palm branches, out of Great Tribulation
11:1–2	Earth	John to measure temple and altar	Worshipers while outer court trampled for 42 months
11:3–12	Earth/heaven	Two witnesses/prophets killed by Beast but taken up in cloud	Prophesy 1,260 days in sackcloth
12:10–12	Heaven	Martyrs rejoice because Dragon hurled down	Victorious through blood of the Lamb and word of their testimony
13:7–10	Earth	Beast conquers saints	Some imprisoned or killed by the sword
14:1–5	Heaven (Mount Zion)	144,000 sing new song before the throne	Name of Lamb and Father on their foreheads, virgins, firstfruits, not liars, blameless
15:2–4	Heaven (sea of glass)	Victors sing song of Moses and Lamb	Hold harps, victorious over Beast, his image, and his number
16:5–7	Heaven (from altar)	Voices acclaim justice of God's bowl judgments	Blood shed by saints and prophets avenged by God's wrath
19:1–3	Heaven	Great multitude shouting "Hallelujah"	Blood shed by servants avenged by Babylon's destruction
19:6–9	Heaven	Great multitude heralds arrival of wedding supper of Lamb	Saints dressed in fine linen, bright and clean
19:11–21	Heaven/earth	Armies follow Rider into battle against Beast and kings	Riding white horses, dressed in fine linen
20:4–6	Heaven	Souls of beheaded come to life and reign for 1,000 years in first resurrection	Seated on thrones, held to testimony of Jesus and word of God, without Beast's mark on forehead or hand

20:9	Earth	Camp/city surrounded by Satan and his followers	Saints/city who are beloved
21:1–4	New heaven/new earth	Holy City, New Jerusalem descending from God	Dressed as bride; people of God never again to experience death, mourning, crying, or pain
21:9–20	New heaven/new earth	Bride, wife of Lamb revealed	Holy City, Jerusalem descending from God and shining with God's glory as precious stones

37. Wars and Battles in Revelation

	Protagonist	Enemy	Result
2:16	One with sharp, double-edged sword	Balaamites and Nicolaitans	Jesus' victory presumed
9:7–10	Locusts	Earth dwellers	People tormented for five months
9:13–19	200 million troops released by four angels	Earth dwellers	A third of humanity killed by three plagues
11:7	Beast from Abyss	Two witnesses	Witnesses killed and bodies left unburied
12:7–9	Michael and his angels	Dragon and his angels	Dragon and his angels hurled from heaven to earth
12:13–16	Dragon	Woman	Woman protected in desert for 3½ times
12:17	Dragon	Woman's offspring	Dragon's victory presumed
13:7–10	Beast	Saints	Saints conquered and killed
16:14	Kings of the earth	God Almighty	Kings' defeat at Armageddon presumed
17:12–14	Beast and ten kings	Lamb and his followers	Lamb overcomes them
19:11–21	Rider on white horse and his army	Beast, kings of the earth, and their armies	Beast and False Prophet captured and destroyed; kings and armies killed and devoured by birds
20:8	Satan and the nations	Saints	Heavenly fire devours the nations; Devil destroyed

38. Theories of the Rapture from Revelation

Pretribulation (4:1)	Prewrath (6:16–17)	Midtribulation (11:12)	Posttribulation (14:16; 17:14; 19:14; 20:4)
John's going up to heaven a type of the rapture	Rapture to occur after opening of the sixth seal and Great Tribulation (7:14)	Two witnesses going up to heaven a type of the rapture	Harvest, army, and enthroned martyrs comprised of both raptured and resurrected followers
Believers to be kept from the hour of trial (3:10)	Great heavenly multitude (7:9–17) is the raptured church that was sealed (7:1–8)	Believers experience trials of first 3½ years of Tribulation	Believers experience Great Tribulation for 42 months/1,260 days (11:2–3; 12:6)
Believers to be exempt from God's wrath (6:16–17)	Believers to be spared God's wrath (6:16–17) because of promise to Philadelphia church (3:10)	Believers spared God's wrath in last 3½ years of Great Tribulation	Believers sealed from wrath of the Lamb (7:3; cf. 14:9–12)
No mention of the church in Rev. 4–18 during Great Tribulation	Opening of seventh seal (8:1) inaugurates Day of the Lord	Seventh trumpet (11:15–19) equated with trumpet of God (1 Thess. 4:16)	Believers are present throughout Rev. and called other names besides "church"
	God's wrath occurs during final half of 42 months		Great multitude in heaven has come out of the Great Tribulation (7:14)
			Churches in Smyrna (2:10) and Pergamum (2:13) experienced tribulation

39. Heavenly Throne-Room Vision
with Parallels in Daniel

Element	Revelation 4–5	Daniel 7
Introductory vision phraseology	4:1ff.	7:1ff.
Thrones set in heaven	4:2, 4	7:9
God sitting on a throne	4:2	7:9
God's appearance on the throne	4:3	7:9
Dressed in white	4:4	7:9
Fire before the throne	4:5	7:9–10
Image of a sea	4:6	7:2–3
Four living creatures/beasts seen	4:6–9	7:3–7
Scroll/books opened	5:2–5, 9	7:10
Vision causes emotional distress in seer	5:4	7:15
Seer receives an explanation from a heavenly servant	5:5	7:16–27
Divine messianic figure approaches the throne	5:6–7	7:13
Kingdom's scope is all peoples, nations, and tongues	5:9	7:14
Saints given divine authority to reign over a kingdom	5:10	7:18, 22, 27
Myriads of angels around the throne	5:11	7:10
Lamb/Son of Man receives power and glory	5:12–13	7:14
Concluding mention of God's eternal reign	5:13	7:27

40. Four Living Creatures with Background in Ezekiel and Isaiah

Revelation	Ezekiel 1	Ezekiel 10	Isaiah 6
In heaven (4:1)	In heaven (1:1)	On earth (10:20)	In heaven (6:1)
Around throne (4:6; 5:6; 14:3)	Around throne (1:26)		Around throne (6:1)
Rainbow mentioned (4:3)	Rainbow mentioned (1:28)		
Four living creatures (4:6)	Four living creatures (1:5–24)	Four living creatures/cherubim (10:15–22)	Seraphim (6:2)
Sea of glass like crystal (4:6)	Expanse appearing like crystal (1:22)	Expanse overhead (10:1)	
Bodies covered with eyes (4:6)	Wheels full of eyes (1:18)	Bodies and wheels covered with eyes (10:12)	
First creature like a lion (4:7)	Four faces: face of a man (1:10)	Four faces: face of a cherub (10:14)	
Second like an ox (4:7)	Face of a lion (1:10)	Face of a man (10:14)	
Third with a face of a man (4:7)	Face of an ox (1:10)	Face of a lion (10:14)	
Fourth like a flying eagle (4:7)	Face of an eagle (1:10)	Face of an eagle (10:14)	
Six wings (4:8)	Four wings (1:6, 11)	Four wings (10:21)	Six wings (6:2)
Eyes under the wings (4:8)		Wings full of eyes (10:12)	
Say, "Holy, holy, holy is the Lord God Almighty" (4:8)	Wings sound like voice of the Almighty (1:24)	Wings sound like voice of God Almighty (10:5)	Say, "Holy, holy, holy is the Lord Almighty" (6:3)
Fall down before the Lamb, God (5:8; 19:4)			
Hold bowls of incense: the prayers of the saints (5:8)	Appearance like burning coals of fire (1:13)	Cherub hands fire to man wearing sacred robe (10:7–8 LXX)	Seraph holds live coal from the altar (6:6)
Surrounded by angels (5:11; 7:11)			
Say, "Amen" (5:14; 19:4)			
Each says in voice like thunder, "Come" (6:1, 3, 5, 7)	Wings sound like rushing waters, tumult of an army (1:24)		Voices shake doorpost and thresholds (6:4)
At the temple (15:6)		In the temple (10:3–5)	In the temple (6:1)
One gives seven angels seven golden bowls (15:7)			
Temple full of smoke (15:8)			Temple full of smoke (6:4)
Say, "Hallelujah!" (19:4)			

41. Identification of the Four Living Creatures with the Gospels

	Irenaeus	Victorinus	Augustine	Athanasius	Modern
Lion	John	Mark	Matthew	Luke	Matthew (royalty)
Ox	Luke	Luke	Luke	Mark	Mark (servanthood)
Man	Matthew	Matthew	Mark	Matthew	Luke (humanity)
Eagle	Mark	John	John	John	John (deity)

42. Hymns of Revelation

Text		Voice(s)	Action	Content	Object	Literary Form
1:5–6		John		Glory and power for saving acts	Jesus Christ	Doxology
4:8	**1st**	4 living creatures	Speak ceaselessly	Thrice holy is God of all time	Lord God Almighty	Sanctus/Trisagion
4:11	↓	24 elders	Fall down, cast crowns before throne	Worthy for creating all things	Lord and God	Acclamation
5:9–10	**2nd**	4 living creatures, 24 elders	Fall down, sing	Worthy to open seals because he was slain	Lamb	Acclamation (new song)
5:12	↓	Angels, elders, living creatures	Speak loudly	Worthy to receive sevenfold attributes	Lamb	Acclamation
5:13	↓	Every creature	Speaks	Praise, honor, glory, and power	God and Lamb	Doxology
5:14	↓	4 living creatures	Speak	Amen	God and Lamb	Amen
7:10	**3rd**	Great multitude	Cries loudly	Salvation	God and Lamb	Victory hymn
7:12	↓	Angels	Fall on faces, worship	Sevenfold attributes	God	Doxology
11:15	**4th**	Heavenly voices	Speak loudly	Kingdom of world now kingdom of God	Lord and Christ	Victory hymn
11:17–18	↓	24 elders	Fall on faces, worship	Thanks for reigning, judging, and rewarding	Lord God Almighty	Thanksgiving
12:10–12	**5th**	Heavenly voice	Speaks loudly	Victors' triumph over Dragon	God and Christ	Victory hymn
14:3		144,000	Sing	Redemption	Lamb	New song not given
15:3–4		Victors	Play harps, sing	Deeds great and marvelous; ways just and true	Lord God Almighty	Praise hymn
16:5–6	**6th**	Angel	Speaks	Just in his judgments	Holy One	Praise hymn
16:7	↓	Martyrs	Speak	True and just in judgments	Lord God Almighty	Amen
19:1–2	**7th**	Great multitude	Shouts	Hallelujah for justice of God's judgments	God	Doxology
19:3	↓	Great multitude	Shouts	Hallelujah for Babylon's destruction	God	Victory hymn

19:4	↓	24 elders, 4 living creatures	Fall down, worship	Hallelujah	God	Amen
19:5	↓	Voice from throne	Speaks	Command for servants to praise God	God	Praise summons
19:6–8	↓	Great multitude	Shouts	Hallelujah for arrival of wedding of the Lamb	Lord God Almighty	Praise hymn

43. Four Horsemen of the Apocalypse with Background in Zechariah

Horse(s)	Revelation 6	Zechariah 1:8	Zechariah 6:2–3
	Riders	Riders	Chariots
1	White (6:2)	Red	Red
2	Red (6:4)	Red	Black
3	Black (6:5)	Dappled grey	White
4	Grey (6:8)	White	Dappled grey
Purpose	Riders permitted to kill one-fourth of earth's inhabitants by war, famine, pestilence, and wild beasts (6:8)	Riders are messengers who return from patrolling the world and find rest and peace everywhere (1:10–11)	Chariots are four spirits/ winds sent to patrol the four directions; northbound chariot gives rest to the north (6:5–8)

Charts on the Book of Revelation

44. Seven Seals and the Apocalypses
in the Synoptic Gospels

Revelation 6	Matthew 24	Mark 13	Luke 21
Seal 1. Conqueror as false Christ (vv. 1–2)	False Christs (vv. 4–5)	False Christs (vv. 5–6)	False Christs (v. 8)
Seal 2. War (vv. 3–4)	Wars (vv. 6–7a)	Wars (vv. 7–8a)	Wars (vv. 9–10)
Seal 3. Famine (vv. 5–6)	Famines (v. 7b)	Earthquakes (v. 8b)	Earthquakes (v. 11a)
Seal 4. Death [Pestilence] (vv. 7–8)	Earthquakes (v. 7b)	Famines (v. 8b)	Famines (v. 11a)
Seal 5. Persecution (vv. 9–11)	Persecutions (vv. 9–10)	Persecutions (vv. 9, 11–13)	Pestilences (v. 11a)
Seal 6. Earthquake, solar eclipse, ensanguinal moon, stars falling, sky rolling up (vv. 12–14)	Solar and lunar eclipse, stars falling, heavenly bodies shaken (v. 29)	Solar and lunar eclipse, stars falling, heavenly bodies shaken (vv. 24–25)	Solar, lunar, and astral signs, heavenly bodies shaken (vv. 11b, 25–26)
Seal 7. Heavenly silence (8:1)	Son of Man comes (v. 30)	Son of Man comes (v. 26)	Persecutions (vv. 12–17)
			Son of Man comes (v. 27)

45. Possible Interrelationships Among the Seals, Trumpets, and Bowls

I. Simultaneous Perspective

Seals	1		2		3		4		5		6			7
Trumpets	1		2		3		4		5		6			7
Bowls	1		2		3		4		6		6			7

II. Sequential Perspective

Seals	1	2	3	4	5	6	7														
Trumpets								1	2	3	4	5	6	7							
Bowls															1	2	3	4	5	6	7

III. Partial Recapitulation Perspective

Seals	1		2		3		4		5		6			7
Trumpets							1		2	3	4		5	6	7
Bowls											1	2	3	4	5	6	7

IV. Telescoping Perspective

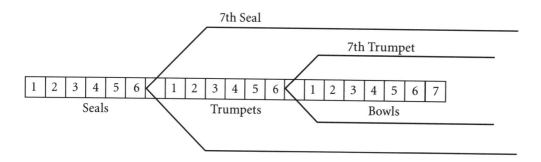

46. Biblical Lists of the Twelve Tribes of Israel

Rev. 7:4–8	Gen. 49:2–28	Num. 1:5–15	Num. 2:3–31	Deut. 33:6–25	Ezek. 48:1–29
Judah	Reuben	Reuben	Judah	Reuben	Dan
Reuben	Simeon	Simeon	Issachar	Judah	Asher
Gad	Levi	Judah	Zebulun	Levi	Naphtali
Asher	Judah	Issachar	Reuben	Benjamin	Manasseh
Naphtali	Zebulun	Zebulun	Simeon	Joseph	Ephraim
Manasseh	Issachar	Joseph	Gad	Ephraim	Reuben
Simeon	Dan	Ephraim[1]	Ephraim	Manasseh	Judah
Levi	Gad	Manasseh[2]	Manasseh	Zebulun	Levi
Issachar	Asher	Benjamin	Benjamin	Issachar	Benjamin
Zebulun	Naphtali	Dan	Dan	Gad	Simeon
Joseph	Joseph	Asher	Asher	Dan	Issachar
Benjamin	Benjamin	Gad	Naphtali	Naphtali	Zebulun
		Naphtali		Asher	Gad

---

1. Ephraim and Manasseh were the sons of Joseph whom Jacob adopted as his own (Gen. 48:5).
2. See note 1 above.

47. Trumpet and Bowl Judgments Compared to the Egyptian Plagues

Seven Trumpets (Rev. 8–9)	Ten Plagues (Exod. 7–11)	Seven Bowls (Rev. 16)
1. Earth hit with hail, fire, and blood (8:7)	6. Boils (9:8–11) 7. Hail (9:13–34)	1. People with Beast's mark afflicted with sores (16:2)
2. 1/3 of sea turned to blood and 1/3 of sea creatures die (8:8–9)	1. Blood (7:14–21)	2. Sea turned to blood and all sea creatures die (16:3)
3. 1/3 of fresh waters embittered by Wormwood (8:11)	1. Blood (7:14–21)	3. Rivers and springs turned to blood (16:4)
4. 1/3 of sun, moon, and stars darkened (8:12)	9. Darkness (10:21–23)	4. Sun scorches people with fire (16:8–9)
5. Locusts released on earth after Abyss is opened (9:1–11)	8. Locusts (10:3–19) 9. Darkness (10:21–23)	5. Darkness on earth and sores break out (16:10–11)
6. 200 million troops at Euphrates River released by 4 angels (9:13–16)	2. Frogs (8:2–14)	6. Kings from east gathered to Euphrates River by 3 unclean spirits resembling frogs (16:12–13)
7. Heavenly temple opens, accompanied by lightning, earthquake, and hail (11:15, 19)	7. Hail (9:18–34)	7. Lightning, severe earthquake, and plague of large hail (16:18–21)
	Egyptians wail loudly because of loss of firstborn (12:30)	People curse God because of the plagues (16:9, 21)
Survivors of plagues refuse to repent (9:20–21)	Pharaoh hardens heart (7:22; 8:15, 19, 32; 9:7, 12, 34–35; 10:20, 27; 11:10)	Survivors of plagues refuse to repent (16:9, 11)

48. Vice Lists in Revelation Correlated to the Ten Commandments

10 Commandments (Exodus)	9:20–21	21:8	22:15	Other Uses in Revelation
1st—20:3	False worship			13:4, 8, 12, 15; 14:9; 16:2
2nd—20:4–5	Idolatry	Idolaters	Idolaters	2:14, 20
6th—20:13	Murders	Murderers	Murderers	
	Sorcery	Sorcerers	Sorcerers	18:23
7th—20:14	Fornication	Fornicators	Fornicators	2:14, 20, 21; 14:8; 17:1–2, 4; 18:3, 9; 19:2
8th—20:15	Thefts			
		Cowards		
		Faithless		
		Abominators	Dogs	21:27
9th—20:16		Liars	Liars	2:2; 3:9; neg.–14:5; 21:27

49. Identification of the Two Witnesses

Views	Prophetic View	Messianic View	Apocalyptic View	Baptist View	Historical View
Identifications	Moses & Elijah (Mal. 4:4–5; Matt. 17:3–4)	Joshua & Zerubbabel (Zech. 3:1–4:14)	Enoch & Elijah	Elijah (Mal. 4:5) & John the Baptist (Matt. 11:14; 17:10–13 para; Luke 1:17; contra John 1:21–24)	Peter & Paul
Activities					
Prophesy 1,260 days clothed in sackcloth (11:3)				John (Matt. 3:4 para)	
Two olive trees and two lampstands who stand before Lord of earth (11:4)		Joshua & Zerubbabel (Zech. 4:3, 11–14)		John the light (John 5:35)	
Fire comes from mouths devouring their enemies (11:5)	Moses (Num. 11:1–3; 16:35); Elijah (1 Kings 18:38; 2 Kings 1:9–12)				
Power to stop rain for 3½ years, power to turn waters to blood, and power to strike earth with plagues (11:6)	Elijah (1 Kings 17:1; 18:1; cf. Luke 4:25; James 5:17) & Moses (Exod. 7:14–24; 8:1–11:10)				
Killed by Beast and bodies lie publicly in great city (11:7–8)			Enoch & Elijah	John the Baptist (Matt. 14:9–12 para)	Peter & Paul (*1 Clem.* 5:2)
Refused burial for 3½ days, then Spirit of life enters them, and they go up to heaven in a cloud (11:11–12)	Elijah (2 Kings 2:11)		Enoch (Gen. 5:24) & Elijah (2 Kings 2:11)		Peter (*1 Clem.* 5:4) & Paul (*1 Clem.* 5:7)

50. Time Periods of Persecution

Time Periods	Holy Participants	Unholy Participants	Outcome
Short time (χρόνον μικρόν; 6:11)	Servants and brothers of souls who were slain	Earth dwellers	Fellow servants and brothers to be killed
Time has run out (χρόνος οὐκέτι; 10:6)	Servants the prophets		Mystery of God accomplished
42 months (11:2)	Holy City	Gentiles	Holy City trampled
1,260 days (11:3)	Two witnesses	Beast	Two witnesses killed
1,260 days (12:6)	Woman	Dragon/Serpent/Devil/Satan	Woman flees to desert for protection
Short time (ὀλίγον καιρὸν; 12:12)	Woman	Devil/Dragon	Dragon pursues woman
Time, times, and half a time (12:14)	Woman	Dragon/Serpent	Woman protected from Serpent
42 months (13:5)	Saints	Beast	Beast wars against saints, conquering them
1,000 years (20:2–6)	Souls of beheaded judge from thrones during respite from persecution	Dragon/Serpent/Devil/Satan	Souls of beheaded reign; Satan bound
Short time (μικρὸν χρόνον; 20:3)	Camp of God's people (20:9)	Satan and nations	Nations surround beloved city but are consumed by fire from heaven

51. Fall of Satan in Revelation

Fall to Earth (12:1–17)	Fall to Lake of Fire (20:1–10)
Conflict precipitated by coming of male child with iron scepter (vv. 4–5)	Conflict precipitated by coming of Rider on white horse with iron scepter (19:11, 15)
Residence in heaven (v. 7)	Residence on earth (implied in v. 1)
Battle with Michael and his angels (v. 7)	Angel seizes Dragon without battle (v. 2)
Dragon and his angels defeated (v. 8)	Dragon bound for 1,000 years (v. 2)
Dragon also called ancient Serpent, Devil, or Satan (v. 9)	Dragon also called ancient Serpent, Devil, or Satan (v. 2)
Dragon's mission to deceive the world (v. 9)	Dragon kept from deceiving the nations (v. 3)
Dragon and his angels cast to earth (v. 9)	Dragon cast into sealed Abyss (v. 3)
Accusation of believers before God ends because Dragon hurled down to earth (v. 10)	Deception of nations ends because dragon locked in Abyss for 1,000 years (vv. 3, 7)
Saints may die but triumph by Lamb's blood and their testimony (vv. 11, 17)	Saints beheaded because of testimony of Jesus and word of God (v. 4)
Dragon's time is short (v. 12)	Dragon set free for a short time (v. 3)
Dragon wars against woman's offspring (v. 17)	Satan with nations war against camp of the saints (vv. 8–9)
	Fire from heaven devours Gog and Magog (vv. 8–9)
	Devil thrown into lake of fire to join Beast and False Prophet (v. 10)

52. Calculating the Number of the Beast (Gematria)

Number	Hebrew	Greek (upper and lower case)
1	א	Αα
2	ב	Ββ
3	ג	Γγ
4	ד	Δδ
5	ה	Εε
6	ו	Ϝ
7	ז	Ζζ
8	ח	Ηη
9	ט	Θθ
10	י	Ιι
20	כ	Κκ
30	ל	Λλ
40	מ	Μμ
50	נ	Νμ
60	ס	Ξξ
70	ע	Οο
80	פ	Ππ
90	צ	Ϙ
100	ק	Ρρ
200	ר	Σσ
300	ש	Ττ
400	ת	Υυ
500	ק ת	Φφ
600	ר ת	Χχ
700	ש ת	Ψψ
800	ת ת	Ωω
900	ק ת ת	ϡ

53. Two Marks of Revelation

Seal of the Living God (7:2–3; 9:4)

OT Background	Taw Mark	Representation	Symbolism
Ezek. 9:4	הַתָּיו; τοῦ θαῦ	X or †	X(ριστός)—Christ

666: The Mark, or Number, of the Beast (13:17–18)

Neron Kaisar	Nero Kaisar	Domitian	Lateinos	Jesus
נ = 50　N	נ = 50　N	A　　= 1	Λ = 30	
ר = 200　R	ר = 200　R	ΚΑΙ　= 31	α = 1	I = 10　I
ו = 6　O	ו = 6　O	ΔΟΜΕΤ = 419	τ = 300	η = 8　E
ן = 50　N		ΣΕΒ　= 207	ε = 5	σ = 200　S
ק = 100　K	ק = 100　K	ΓΕ　　= 8	ι = 10	o = 70　O
ס = 60　S	ס = 60　S	666	ν = 50	υ = 400　U
ר = 200　R	ר = 200　R		o = 70	ς = 200　S
666	616 (var)		ς = 200	888
			666	

54. Thematic Parallels Between the Beast of Revelation and the Beasts of Daniel

Description	Revelation	Daniel
Comes up from the Abyss/sea	11:7; 13:1; 17:8	7:3
Makes war, conquers and kills the saints	11:7; 13:7, 10, 15	7:8 (LXX), 21, 25
Has ten horns	13:1; cf. 12:3	7:7, 20
Resembles a leopard	13:2	7:6
Resembles a bear	13:2	7:5
Resembles a lion	13:2	7:4
Given power and authority by Dragon	13:2, 4, 5, 7	7:6
Wounded fatally	13:3, 12, 14	7:11
Speaks great things with mouth	13:5	7:8, 20
Blasphemes God	13:5, 6	7:25; cf. 11:36
Rules for 42 months (time, times, and half a time)	13:5; cf. 12:14	7:25
Ten horns are ten kings	17:3, 7, 12, 16	7:24
Goes to destruction	17:8, 11	7:11, 26
Thrown into fire	19:20; 20:10	7:11

55. Portrait of the Beast in Revelation

11:7	13:1–18	16:2–16	17:3–17	19:17–21
			Was (vv. 8, 11)	
			Is not (vv. 8, 11)	
Comes up from the Abyss	Comes up from the sea (v. 1)		Is to come up from the Abyss (v. 8)	
	Has 10 horns (v. 1)		Has 10 horns, which = 10 kings (vv. 3, 7, 12, 16)	
	Has 7 heads (v. 1)		Has 7 heads (vv. 3, 7)	
			7 heads = 7 hills and 7 kings (vv. 9–10)	
	Has blasphemous names on its heads (v. 1)		Full of blasphemous names (v. 3)	
	Looks like leopard, feet like bear, mouth like lion (v. 2)		Woman dressed in scarlet and purple sits/rides on him (vv. 3, 7)	
	Dragon gives him his power, throne, and great authority (v. 2)	Fifth bowl poured on his throne (v. 10)		
	One of his heads appeared fatally wounded by the sword, but he lived (vv. 3, 12, 14)			
	Fatal wound healed (vv. 3, 12)			
	Whole earth amazed and followed him (v. 3)		Inhabitants of earth amazed at sight of him (v. 8)	
	People worshiped Dragon and him (v. 4)			
	Permitted to say proud and blasphemous words against God and those dwelling in heaven (vv. 5, 6)			
			Is an eighth king (v. 11)	
	Exercises authority for 42 months (v. 5)		Receives authority for one hour with 10 kings (v. 12)	

Wars against, conquers, and kills 2 witnesses	Fights against saints and conquers them (v. 7)			
	Given authority over every tribe, people, language, and nation (v. 7)		Waters are peoples, multitudes, nations, and languages (v. 15)	
	All inhabitants of the earth worship him (vv. 8, 12)		All inhabitants of earth will be astonished at him (v. 8)	
	Those whose names not written in Book of Life worship him (v. 8)		Those whose names not written in Book of Life astonished (v. 8)	
	Beast out of earth exercises authority on his behalf (v. 12)			
	Beast out of earth orders his image to be erected (v. 14)	First bowl poured out on those who worship his image (v. 2)		False Prophet deluded those who worshiped his image (v. 20)
	His image comes alive and speaks (v. 15)	Evil spirit looking like a frog comes out of his mouth (v. 13)		
	Earth dwellers marked with his name or number (vv. 16–17; cf. 14:9, 11; 20:4)	First bowl poured out on those with his mark (v. 2)		False Prophet deluded those who received his mark (v. 20)
	His number is a man's: 666 (v. 18)			
		Evil spirits gather kings of earth for battle (v. 14) at Armageddon (v. 16)	10 kings give their power and authority to him (vv. 13, 17)	He and kings of earth gather and fight the Rider and his army (v. 19)
			He and 10 kings fight against the Lamb (v. 14)	
			Lamb will conquer them (v. 14)	Captured with False Prophet (v. 20)
			He and 10 horns will hate, strip, eat, and burn the prostitute (v. 16)	
			Headed for destruction (vv. 8, 11)	Thrown alive into lake of fire with False Prophet (v. 20; cf. 20:10)

56. Rise and Demise of the Evil Trinity

A   Dragon (12:3)

    B   Sea-Beast (13:1)

        C   Earth-Beast = False Prophet (13:11)

            D   Babylon (14:8)

                E   Beast-Worshipers (14:9)

                E'   Beast-Worshipers (16:2)

            D'   Babylon (16:19)

        C'   Earth-Beast = False Prophet (19:20)

    B'   Sea-Beast (19:20)

A'   Dragon (20:2)

57. Worship of the Emperor—the Beast of Revelation 13:4— Contrasted with Divine Worship

Imperial Attribute	Sources	Divine Counterpart in Revelation
Son of God	*IGR* 4.1756	2:18
Morning star	*Silv.* 4.1	2:28; 22:16
Holy	Martial Statius, Ovid	3:7; 6:10; 15:4; 16:5
Beginning of breath and life	*OGIS* 458	3:14
Honor	*OGIS* 458	4:9; 5:13; 7:12
Lord and God (*dominus et deus*)	*Epig.* 5.8.1; 7.34.8; 9.66.3; *Dom.* 13.2	4:11
Power	*Epig.* 9.61	
Glory	*Epig.* 1.16	4:11; 5:12, 13; 7:12; 19:1, 7
Worthy	*Silv.* 1.4.123; *J.W.* 7.71	5:12
Master (δεσπότης)	Cassius Dio 67.5.7; 67.13.4; *Or.* 45.1	6:10
Savior	*J.W.* 7.71; *OGIS* 668.3	7:10; 12:10; 19:1 (σωτηρία)
Lord of all the world	*SIG*³ 814.32	11:4

58. Four *Hōde* (ῶδε "Here") Sayings of Revelation

Reference	Speaker	Literary Form	Audience	Message
13:10	Heavenly voice (Jesus or angel?)	With hearing saying, "He who has an ear [οὖς], let him hear" (13:9; cf. 2:7, 11, 17, 29; 3:6, 13, 22)	Saints	Called to endurance and faithfulness
13:18	Heavenly voice (Jesus or angel?)	Modified hearing saying; mind (νοῦς) instead of ear (οὖς)	Saints (implied)	Wisdom to calculate the number of the beast, 666
14:12	Angel	Precedes second beatitude and direct speech by Holy Spirit (14:13)	Saints	Called to endurance: keeping God's commandments and faithfulness to Jesus
17:9–11	Angel	Modified hearing saying; mind (νοῦς) instead of ear (οὖς)	John	Wisdom to understand the meaning of the seven hills and seven kings

59. Paired Angelic Revelations in Revelation

17:1–19:10	21:9–22:9
17:1 Καὶ ἦλθεν εἷς ἐκ τῶν ἑπτὰ ἀγγέλων Then came one of the seven angels	21:9 Καὶ ἦλθεν εἷς ἐκ τῶν ἑπτὰ ἀγγέλων Then came one of the seven angels
τῶν ἐχόντων τὰς ἑπτὰ φιάλας who had the seven bowls	τῶν ἐχόντων τὰς ἑπτὰ φιάλας who had the seven bowls
καὶ ἐλάλησεν μετ' ἐμοῦ λέγων· and he spoke with me saying,	καὶ ἐλάλησεν μετ' ἐμοῦ λέγων· and he spoke with me saying,
δεῦρο, δείξω σοι "Come, I will show you	δεῦρο, δείξω σοι "Come, I will show you
τὸ κρίμα τῆς πόρνης τῆς μεγάλης the judgment of the great prostitute . . ."	τὴν νύμφην τὴν γυναῖκα τοῦ ἀρνίου. the bride, the wife of the Lamb."
17:3 καὶ ἀπήνεγκέν με Then he carried me away	21:10 καὶ ἀπήνεγκέν με Then he carried me away
εἰς ἔρημον ἐν πνεύματι. into a desert in the Spirit.	ἐν πνεύματι ἐπὶ ὄρος μέγα καὶ ὑψηλόν, in the Spirit to a large and high mountain
Καὶ εἶδον (cf. 17:6) Then I saw	καὶ ἔδειξέν μοι Then he showed me
γυναῖκα καθημένην 17:5 Βαβυλὼν ἡ μεγάλη a woman sitting . . . Babylon the great	τὴν πόλιν τὴν ἁγίαν Ἰερουσαλὴμ καταβαίνουσαν the Holy City Jerusalem coming down
17:3 ἔχων κεφαλὰς ἑπτὰ καὶ κέρατα δέκα . . . 17:4 ἔχουσα ποτήριον χρυσοῦν having seven heads and ten horns . . . having a golden cup	21:11 ἔχουσαν τὴν δόξαν τοῦ θεοῦ . . . 21:12 ἔχουσα τεῖχος μέγα καὶ ὑψηλόν, ἔχουσα πυλῶνας δώδεκα . . . having the glory of God . . . having a large and high wall, having twelve gates . . .
{Body of vision}	{Body of vision}
17:7 Καὶ εἶπέν μοι ὁ ἄγγελος· Then the angel said to me,	21:15 Καὶ ὁ λαλῶν μετ' ἐμοῦ . . . Then the one who was speaking with me . . .
18:1 εἶδον . . . I saw . . .	22:1 Καὶ ἔδειξέν μοι . . . Then he showed me . . .
19:9 Καὶ λέγει μοι· Then he said to me,	22:6 Καὶ εἶπέν μοι· Then he said to me,
οὗτοι οἱ λόγοι ἀληθινοὶ τοῦ θεοῦ εἰσιν. "These words of God are true	οὗτοι οἱ λόγοι πιστοὶ καὶ ἀληθινοί, "These words are faithful and true
19:10 καὶ ἔπεσα . . . προσκυνῆσαι αὐτῷ. Then I fell . . . to worship him	22:8 ἔπεσα προσκυνῆσαι I fell to worship
ἔμπροσθεν τῶν ποδῶν αὐτου before his feet	ἔμπροσθεν τῶν ποδῶν τοῦ ἀγγέλου before the feet of the angel
καὶ λέγει μοι· Then he said to me,	22:9 καὶ λέγει μοι· Then he said to me,
ὅρα μή· "Do not do that!	ὅρα μή· "Do not do that!
σύνδουλός σού εἰμι I am your fellow servant	σύνδουλός σού εἰμι I am your fellow servant
καὶ τῶν ἀδελφῶν σου and of your brothers	καὶ τῶν ἀδελφῶν σου τῶν προφητῶν and of your brothers the prophets

τῶν ἐχόντων τὴν μαρτυρίαν Ἰησοῦ· who are holding the testimony of Jesus	καὶ τῶν τηρούντων τοὺς λόγους τοῦ βιβλίου τούτου· who are keeping the words of this book.
τῷ θεῷ προσκύνησον. Worship God!	τῷ θεῷ προσκύνησον. Worship God!

60. Historical Identification of the Seven Emperors (Rev. 17:9–11) in Relationship to the Twelve Caesars

	Name	Family	Date of Reign
		Julio-Claudians	
1.	Julius Caesar		49–44 B.C.
2.	(Octavian) Augustus		(31–) 27 B.C.–A.D. 14
3.	Tiberius		A.D. 14–37
4.	Gaius (Caligula)		A.D. 37–41
5.	Claudius		A.D. 41–54
6.	Nero		A.D. 54–68
		Civil War Emperors	
7.	Galba		A.D. 68–69
8.	Otho		A.D. 69
9.	Vitellius		A.D. 69
		Flavians	
10.	Vespasian		A.D. 69–79
11.	Titus		A.D. 79–81
12.	Domitian		A.D. 81–96

Historic	Principate	Despotic	Antichrist	Tyrannical
Five fallen	*Five fallen*	*Five fallen*	*Five fallen*	*Five fallen*
1. Julius	1. Augustus	1. Augustus	1. Nero	1. Julius
2. Augustus	2. Tiberius	2. Tiberius	2. Galba	2. Gaius
3. Tiberius	3. Gaius	3. Gaius	3. Otho	3. Claudius
4. Gaius	4. Claudius	4. Claudius	4. Vitellius	4. Nero
5. Claudius	5. Nero	5. Nero	5. Vespasian	5. Domitian
One is	*One is*	*One is*	*One is*	*One is*
6. Nero	6. Galba	6. Vespasian	6. Titus	6. Nerva
One not yet	*One not yet*	*One not yet*	*One not yet*	*One not yet*
7. Galba	7. Otho	7. Titus	7. Domitian	7. Trajan
8. Otho	8. Nero	8. Domitian	8. Unidentified	8. Unidentified

Christological	Empires
Five fallen	*Five fallen*
1. Gaius	1. Egypt
2. Claudius	2. Assyria
3. Nero	3. Babylon
4. Vespasian	4. Persia
5. Titus	5. Greece
One is	*One is*
6. Domitian	6. Rome
One not yet	*One not yet*
7. Unidentified	7. All future empires
8. Unidentified	8. Final anti-Christian empire

61. Trading Products of Revelation 18 in Relationship to Tyre and Rome

List of Products (Rev. 18:12–13)	Sources for Tyre's Products (Ezek. 27:12–24)	Sources of Rome's Products
Gold	Sheba, Raamah (v. 22)	Spain
Silver	Tarshish (v. 12)	Spain
Precious stones	Aram (v. 16); Sheba, Raamah (v. 22)	Asia Minor, India
Pearls		Red Sea, Persian Gulf, India
Fine linen	Aram (v. 16)	Asia Minor, Egypt, Spain
Purple	Aram (v. 16)	Tyre, Asia
Silk		China
Scarlet		Asia Minor
Citron wood		Morocco
Ivory	Rhodes (v. 15)	Africa, India
Costly wood (ebony?)	Rhodes (v. 15)	Africa, India
Bronze	Greece, Tubal, Meschech (v. 13)	Corinth, Spain
Iron	Tarshish (v. 12); Uzal (v. 19)	Pontus, Spain
Marble		Asia, Africa, Greece
Cinnamon (cassia)	Uzal (v. 19); Judah, Israel (v. 17 LXX)	South India, east Africa
Spice	Sheba, Raamah (v. 22)	Pontus, Media, south India
Incense	Judah, Israel (v. 17)	South Arabia
Myrrh		South Arabia, east Africa
Frankincense		South Arabia
Wine	Helbon (v. 18) via Damascus	Asia Minor, Sicily, Spain
Olive oil	Judah, Israel (v. 17)	Asia Minor, Spain, Africa
Fine flour		North Africa, Egypt
Wheat	Minnith (v. 17)	North Africa, Egypt
Cattle		Greece, Sicily
Sheep	Arabia, Kedar (v. 21)	Asia Minor, Sicily
Horses	Beth Togarmah (v. 14)	Cappadocia, Africa, Spain, Greece
Carriages		Gaul
Slaves	Greece, Tubal, Meshech (v. 13)	Asia Minor, Judea, Britain, Germany

62. Last Battle in Revelation

	16:12–21	19:11–21	20:7–10
Title	Great day of God Almighty (v. 14)	Great supper of God (v. 17)	Gog and Magog (v. 8)
Deceivers	Dragon, Beast, and False Prophet (v. 13)	False Prophet (v. 20)	Satan, Devil (vv. 7–8, 10)
Combatants (Unrighteous)	Kings of the earth (v. 14)	Beast, kings of the earth, their armies (v. 19)	Nations (v. 7)
Combatants (Righteous)	Victors (v. 15)	Rider on white horse, his army (v. 19)	Saints (v. 9)
Action	Perform signs (v. 14)	Perform signs (v. 20)	Deceive nations (v. 8)
Divine Action	Gave cup of wrath (v. 19; 6:16–17; 11:18)		
Place	Harmagedon (v. 16)		Camp at beloved city (v. 9)
Angelic Announcement	"It is done" (v. 17)	"Come, gather together . . ." (v. 17)	
Outcome	Great city splits into thirds, other cities collapse, plague of hail (vv. 19–21)	Beast and False Prophet captured and thrown into lake of sulfur (v. 20); kings and armies killed, and eaten by birds (vv. 18, 21)	Nations devoured by fire (v. 9); Devil thrown into lake of sulfur (v. 10); Devil, Beast, and False Prophet tormented forever (v. 10)

63. Messiah as an Eschatological Judge

	Agent	Action	Sphere	Instrument	Genitive Phrase
Rev. 19:15, 21 (cf. 12:5)	Rider (Messiah)	smite	nations	sword	of his mouth
Isa. 11:4	He (Messiah)	smite	earth	rod	of his mouth
Pss. Sol. 17:24, 35	Lord Messiah	destroy (v. 24), smite (v. 35)	nations (v. 24), earth (v. 35)	word	of his mouth
4QpIsa[a]8–10[1]	Root of David	judge	peoples	sword	
1QSb5 24a	Prince	smite	peoples?	might	of your mouth
1QSb5 24b	Prince	devastate	earth	rod	
1QSb5 24–25	Prince	slay	wicked	breath	of your lips
2 Thess. 2:8	Lord Jesus	slay	the wicked one	breath	of his mouth
4 Ezra 13:9–11, 37–38	(God's) Son	destroy (v. 38)	nations (v. 37)	fire (=law v. 38)	from his mouth, lips, tongue
1 En. 62:2	Chosen one	slay	wicked	word (=sword v. 12?)	of his mouth

---

1. This and the three following references below are to manuscripts from the Dead Sea Scrolls.

64. Interpretations of the 1,000 Years from Revelation 20:1–6

Historic Premillenialism	Dispensational Premillenialism	Postmillenialism	Amillenialism	Messianic Age
Future reality	Future reality	Future reality	Present reality	Future reality
Rapture after Tribulation	Rapture of saints before 7-year Tribulation		Rapture after Tribulation	Rapture after Tribulation
2nd coming of Christ with his living and dead saints (19:11–16)	2nd coming of Christ with his saints (19:11–16)	Progress of church between 1st and 2nd comings described (19:11–21)	2nd coming of Christ with his saints (19:11–16), a literary doublet with final judgment (20:11–15)	2nd coming of Christ with living and dead saints (19:11–16), a literary doublet of physical (1st) resurrection of saints who rule with Christ for 1,000 years (20:4–6)
Destruction of Antichrist and his allies (19:17–21)	Destruction of Antichrist and his allies (19:17–21)			Destruction of Antichrist and his allies (19:17–21), a literary doublet with Satan's release and defeat in final eschatological battle (20:7–10)
Satan bound for 1,000 years (20:1–3)	Satan bound for 1,000 years (20:1–3)	Satan bound for 1,000 years (20:1–3) refers to Christianizing of the world	Satan bound for 1,000 years (20:1–3), a literary doublet with defeat of Satan at Christ's 1st coming (12:7–9) and the period between Christ's 1st and 2nd comings	1,000 years in which Satan is bound a metaphor for Lord's return and institution of kingdom (20:1–3); "parousia" or "day of the Lord" not used in Rev.
Physical (1st) resurrection of saints, who rule over earth with Christ for 1,000 years (20:4–6)	Physical (1st) resurrection of saints and institution of millennial earthly kingdom, in which Jews rule for 1,000 years (20:4–6)	Spiritual (1st) resurrection of souls of saints, who reign with Christ in heaven between their death and Christ's 2nd coming (20:4–6; cf. 6:10–11; 7:9–17)	Spiritual (1st) resurrection of souls of saints, who reign with Christ in heaven between their death and Christ's 2nd coming (20:4–6; cf. 6:10–11; 7:9–17)	Ep. of Barnabas (15:4) suggests 6000 years of human history followed by 7th 1,000-year period called by rabbis the messianic age
After 1,000 years Satan loosed and defeated in final eschatological battle (20:7–10)	After 1,000 years Satan loosed and defeated in final eschatological battle (20:7–10)	Every tribe, language, people, and nation shows gradual expansion of Christianized world (5:9; 7:9)		

Resurrection of dead and last judgment (20:11–15)	Resurrection of dead and last judgment (20:11–15)	Second coming of Christ	Resurrection of all dead not separated by 1,000 years; and last judgment (20:11–15)	Resurrection of dead and last judgment (20:11–15)

65. Lists of Jewels in Antiquity

Rev. 21:19–20 (OT list number)	Exod. 28:17–20 LXX; 36:17–20 LXX (39:10–13 MT)	Ezek. 28:13 LXX	Josephus *Ant.* 3.168; *J.W.* 5.234	Zodiac
jasper (6)	1. carnelian	carnelian	sardonyx (carnelian)	amethyst
sapphire (5)	2. topaz	topaz	topaz	jacinth
chalcedony	3. emerald	emerald	emerald	chrysoprase
emerald (3)	4. turquoise	turquoise	turquoise	topaz
sardonyx (12)	5. sapphire	sapphire	jasper	beryl
carnelian (1)	6. jasper	jasper	sapphire	chrysolite
chrysolite (10)	7. jacinth	jacinth	jacinth (agate)	carnelian
beryl (11)	8. agate	agate	amethyst	sardonyx
topaz (2)	9. amethyst	amethyst	agate (jacinth)	emerald
chrysoprase	10. chrysolite	chrysolite	chrysolite (onyx)	chalcedony
jacinth (7)	11. beryl	beryl	onyx (beryl)	sapphire
amethyst (9)	12. onyx	onyx	beryl (chrysolite)	jasper

66. Paradise Motifs in Revelation and the Prophets

Motif	Revelation	Prophets
Peace among animals	5:13	Isa. 11:6–7; 65:25
Peace between humans and animals		Isa. 11:8; Hos. 2:18
Longevity	20:6; 22:5	Isa. 65:20, 22; Zech. 8:4
New heaven and new earth	21:1	Isa. 65:17; 66:22
Fellowship with God	21:3, 7; 22:3	Jer. 31:33; Ezek. 43:7; 48:35; Hos. 2:19–20; Zeph. 3:15–17
No death	21:4	Isa. 25:8; 26:19
No mourning or crying	21:4	Isa. 25:8; 65:19; Jer. 31:13
No disease	21:4; 22:2	Isa. 65:20; Ezek. 47:12; Mal. 4:2
Abundant water	21:6; 22:1, 17	Isa. 35:6–7; 41:18–19; 43:19; 55:1; Ezek. 47:1–12; Joel 3:18; Zech. 14:8
Glory of God present	21:23	Isa. 66:18–19; Ezek. 43:2–5; 44:4
Salvation of the nations	21:24	Isa. 66:20–21
Peace among the nations	21:25	Isa. 2:4; 9:6–7; Hos. 2:18; Mic. 4:3–4; Zech. 9:10
Worship by all nations	21:26	Isa. 2:2–3; 19:21; 66:23
Place of moral purity	21:27; 22:15	Ezek. 36:25; 43:7; Zech. 13:1–2; Mal. 3:2–5
Great fruitfulness	22:2	Isa. 35:1–2; Jer. 31:12; Ezek. 47:12; Hos. 2:22; Joel 3:18; Amos 9:13–14
Curse lifted	22:3	Isa. 65:22–23

67. Death and Resurrection in Revelation 19–22

	First Death (Physical)		Second Death (Eternal)	
		First Resurrection (Physical)		"Second" Life (Eternal)
Saints	20:4 →	19:14; 20:4–6 →		20:15; 21:1–22:5, esp. 21:4, 6; 22:1, 5
Earth dwellers	19:21; 20:9 →	20:5, 12–13 →	19:20; 20:10, 14–15; 21:8; cf. 20:6	

68. Architectural Features of the New Jerusalem

Rev. 21:18–21	Isa. 54:11–12 (MT)	Isa. 54:11–12 (LXX)	Tob. 13:16–18a	5QNJ	Targum Isaiah
streets pure gold	*stones* antimony	*stone* carbuncle	*streets* carbuncle, ophir-stone	*streets* white stone	*pavement-stones* antimony
foundations precious stones	*foundations* sapphires	*foundations* sapphire			*foundations* jewels
	battlements rubies	*battlements* jasper	*battlements* pure gold		*timbers* pearls
gates pearls	*gates* jewels	*gates* crystal stones	*doors* sapphire, emerald	*gates* pearls	*gates* carbuncles
wall jasper	*wall* precious stones	*wall* precious stones	*wall* precious stone		*border* precious stones

69. Literary Parallels Between Revelation's Prologue and Epilogue

Prologue (1:1–8)	Parallel	Epilogue (22:6–21)
1:1	God sends his angel	22:6 (cf. v. 16)
1:1	His servants are shown	22:6
1:1	Things must soon happen	22:6
1:1	John a servant	22:9
1:2	John sees things	22:8
1:2	Testimony of Jesus	22:20
1:3	Blessing given	22:7
1:3	Keeping the words of the prophecy	22:7
1:3	The time is near	22:10
1:4	Seven churches addressed	22:16
1:4–5	Grace from Jesus	22:21
1:4	The Spirit mentioned	22:17
1:6	Freedom from sins	22:14–15
1:7	Jesus coming	22:7, 20
1:8	I am the Alpha and Omega	22:13

70. Benedictions in the New Testament

Reference	Term Χαρις ("Grace")	Source	Beneficiaries
Rom. 16:20	The grace	of our Lord Jesus	be with you
1 Cor. 16:23	The grace	of the Lord Jesus	be with you
2 Cor. 13:14	The grace	of the Lord Jesus Christ	be with you all
Gal. 6:18	The grace	of our Lord Jesus Christ	be with your spirit, brothers and sisters
Eph. 6:24	Grace		be with all who love our Lord Jesus Christ
Phil. 4:23	The grace	of the Lord Jesus Christ	be with your spirit
Col. 4:18	Grace		be with you
1 Thess. 5:28	The grace	of our Lord Jesus Christ	be with you
2 Thess. 3:18	The grace	of our Lord Jesus Christ	be with you all
1 Tim. 6:21	Grace		be with you
2 Tim. 4:22	Grace		be with you
Titus 3:15	Grace		be with you all
Philem. 25	The grace	of our Lord Jesus Christ	be with your spirit
Heb. 13:25	Grace		be with you all
Rev. 22:21	The grace	of the Lord Jesus	be with all the saints

71. Thematic Parallels Between
Genesis 1–3 and Revelation

Thematic Parallel	Genesis	Revelation
Structural use of seven days/seven churches, seals, trumpets, bowls	1:1–2:3	1:11, 20; 2:1–3:22; 5:1, 5; 6:1–8:1; 8:2–11:15; 15:7; 16:1–21
God's creation in the beginning	1:1	3:14
Creation/disappearance of heavens and earth	1:1	21:1
Spirit hovers/carries away	1:2	21:10 (cf. 17:3)
Creation/disappearance of night	1:5	21:25; 22:5
Creation/disappearance of sea	1:10	21:1
Creation/disappearance of sun and moon	1:16	21:23
Humanity to rule/reign	1:26, 28	20:4, 6; 22:5
River flows in garden	2:10	22:1
Introduction/elimination of death	2:17; cf. 3:3, 19	21:4; cf. 2:11; 20:6
Eve/saints prepared as bride	2:22, 24	19:7; 21:2, 9
Satan/Serpent as deceiver	3:1, 13	12:9; 20:3, 8, 10
Fruit grows in garden	3:2–3, 6, 12; cf. 2:16	22:2
Shame in nakedness	3:7, 10–11 (cf. 2:25)	3:18; 16:15
Enmity between Serpent and woman	3:15	12:13–16
Enmity between Serpent and woman's seed	3:15	12:17
Seed to crush Serpent's head	3:15	20:10
Introduction/elimination of pain	3:16	21:4
Introduction/elimination of curse	3:17	22:3
Eve/heavenly woman give birth	3:20	12:5, 13
Denial/permission to tree of life	3:22, 24; cf. 2:9	22:2; cf. 2:7
Denial/permission to Eden (Paradise LXX)	3:23–24	2:7
Banishment/access to God's presence	3:23	22:4
Wrongdoers outside of garden/city	3:24	21:27; 22:15

72. Textual Evidence for Revelation

Manuscripts	Century	Aland Category[1]	Contents
Papyri			
P[98]	2nd	I	1:13–20
P[47]	3rd	I	9:10–11:3; 11:5–16:15; 16:17–17:2
P[18]	3rd	I	1:4–7
P[24]	4th	I	5:5–8; 6:5–8
P[85]	4th–5th	II	9:19–10:2, 5–9
P[43]	6th	II	2:12–13; 15:8–16:2
Uncials			
א (01)	4th	I	1:1–22:21
0169	4th	III	3:19–4:3
0207	4th	III	9:2–15
A (02)	5th	I	1:1–22:21
C (04)	5th	II	1:3–3:19; 6:1–7:13; 8:1–4; 9:17–10:9; 11:4–16:12; 18:3–19:4
0163	5th	III	16:17–20
0229	8th	III	18:16–17; 19:4–6
P (025)	9th	V	1:1–16:11; 17:2–19:20; 20:10–22:5
046	10th	V	1:1–22:21
051	10th	V	11:15–13:1; 13:4–22:7; 22:15–21
052	10th	V	7:16–8:12
Miniscules	9th–19th	I, II, III, V	292 total, 98 are commentaries

Patristic Quotations	Date/Century	Works
Greek Authors		
Hippolytus of Rome	ca. 170–236	*De antichristo; Commentarium in Danielem; Philosophoumena*
Origen	185–254	*Scholia in Apocalypsem*
Oecumenius	6th	*Apocalypse*
Andreas of Caesarea	6th	*Apocalypse*
Latin Authors		
Victorinus of Pettau	died ca. 304	*In Apocalypsin*
Tyconius	ca. 330–90	In *Turin Fragments* possibly
Primasius	6th	*In Apocalypsin*
Beatus of Liébana	died 798	*Commentarius in Apocalypsin*
Greek Lectionaries		*No readings in Revelation*

Versions	Date/Century	Manuscripts
Old Latin (it)	2nd–13th	13
Vulgate (vg)	4th–13th	16 primary
Armenian (arm)	5th–	arm[4] primary
Georgian (geo)	10th–12th	3 primary
Coptic Sahidic (cop[sa])	3rd	1, most are fragments
Coptic Bohairic (cop[bo])	4th	A few
Ethiopic (eth)	550–650	26
Syriac (syr[ph])	507–8	Philoxenian
Syriac (syr[h])	616	Harclean

---

1. Category I: Manuscripts of a very special quality which should always be considered in establishing the original text.

   Category II: Manuscripts of a special quality, but distinguished from manuscripts of Category I by the presence of alien influences.

   Category III: Manuscripts of a distinctive character with an independent text . . . particularly important for the history of the text.

   Category IV: Manuscripts of the D text.

   Category V: Manuscripts with a purely or predominantly Byzantine text.

73. Canonical History of Revelation

Figure	Date/ Century	Status	Writings
Marcion	2C	No	*Apostolikon*
Unknown Roman	2C	Yes	Muratorian Canon
Melito of Sardis	2C	Yes	*Devil and the Apocalypse of John*
Tatian	2C	No	*Oration*
Theophilus of Antioch	2C	Yes	*Against Hermogenes* (lost)
Churches at Lyons and Vienne	3C	Yes	*Epistle of the Churches at Lyons and Vienne*
Irenaeus	2C	Yes	*Against Heresies*
Montanists/Proclus	2C	Yes	Gaius, *Dialogue Against Proclus*
Gaius (Caius)	3C	No	*Dialogue Against Proclus*
Hippolytus of Rome	3C	Yes	*On the Gospel of John and the Apocalypse*
Alogi	3C	No	Epiphanius, *Panarion*
Tertullian	3C	Yes	*Against Marcion, Flight, Modesty*
Clement of Alexandria	3C	Yes	*Stromata*
Origen	3C	Yes	*Expositions on the Gospel to John*
Dionysius	3C	Yes	*On Promises* (but not apostolic)
Cyprian	3C	Yes	*To Fortunatus, Epistle 63*
Unknown Alexandrian	4C	Yes	Codex Claromontanus
Constantine	4C	Yes	Eusebius, *Life of Constantine*
Eusebius	4C	Yes	*Church History* (also "spurious")
Unknown North African	ca. 360	Yes	Cheltenham Canon
Synod of Laodicea	ca. 363	No	Canon 60
Athanasius	367	Yes	Thirty-Ninth Festal Letter
Cyril of Jerusalem	4C	No	*Catechetical Lectures*
Apostolic Canons	ca. 380	No	Canon 85
Amphliochus of Iconium	4C	No	*Iambics for Seleucus*
3rd Council of Carthage	397	Yes	Canon 47
Epiphanius of Salamis	4C	Yes	*Panarion*
Gregory of Nazianzus	4C	No	Poem (1.12.5ff.) ratified by Trullan Synod in 692
Syrian Church	4–5C	No	Peshitta (sustaining Theodore of Mopsuestia)
John Chrysostom	4–5C	No	*Synopsis of Sacred Scripture*
Jerome	4–5C	Yes	*Epistles 53, 129*
Pope Innocent I	405	Yes	*Epistle 6*
Philoxenus	507–8	Yes	Philoxenian Syriac Version
Pope Gelasius?	6C	Yes	*Gelasian Decree*
Nicephorus	9C	No	Stichometry in *Chronography*
Armenian Synod of Constantinople	12C	Yes	New translation sponsored by Nerses, Archbishop of Tarsus

Pope Eugenius IV	1439–43	Yes	Council of Florence (first Catholic affirmation)
Martin Luther	1522	Disputed	German NT (not "apostolic or prophetic")
Ulrich Zwingli	1528	No	Berne Disputation
Johann Brentz	1531	Disputed	Württemburg Confession
Pope Paul III	1546	Yes	Council of Trent
John Calvin	1559	Yes	French Confession of Faith
Guido de Bräs	1561	Yes	Belgic Confession of Faith
Westminster Assembly	1647	Yes	Westminster Confession of Faith

74. Seven Churches Today

Ancient Name	Modern Name	Archaeological Excavation	Local Museum(s)	Main Sites
Ephesus	Selçuk	Austrian	Ephesus Museum	Ancient city with imperial cult temple, theater; Artemisium; St. John's Basilica; Pollio Aqueduct
Smyrna	İzmir	Turkish	Archaeology Museum; Museum of History & Art; City Museum	Agora; acropolis (Kadifekale); Old Smyrna (Tepekule); aqueducts
Pergamum	Bergama	German	Bergama Museum	Acropolis with imperial cult temple, theater; Red Basilica; Asclepion, theater; amphitheater
Thyatira	Akhisar	None	Manisa Museum	Colonnaded street (Mezarlik Tepe)
Sardis	Sart	American	Manisa Museum	Artemis temple; synagogue, gymnasium; acropolis; Lydian burial mounds (Bin Tepe)
Philadelphia	Alaşehir	None	Manisa Museum	Acropolis with stadium; St. John's Church
Laodicea	North of Denizli	Turkish	Hierapolis Museum	Ancient city with theaters, agora, stadium; Roman bridge, water system

75. Map of Roman Province of Asia

ROMAN PROVINCE OF ASIA

Heraclea

Egnatian Way · Byzantium

Nicomedia

BITHYNIA AND PONTUS

Nicea

Dorylaeum

A S I A

Troas

Assos

Mitylene · Pergamum

Thyatira

Sardis

Chios

Philadelphia

Smyrna

Ephesus · Tralles

Hierapolis

Pisidian Antioch · Iconium

SAMOS

Laodicea

LYCIA AND PAMPHYLIA · Lystra

Magnesia · Colossae

PATMOS · Miletus

Cos

Perga

Attalia

Rhodes · Patara · Myra

M E D I T E R R A N E A N   S E A

✠ Seven Churches of Revelation

✠ Town with church

— · — Boundary of Roman province, 65 CE

— Roman road

0   100   200 km

0   40   80   120 miles

76. Map of Imperial Cult Temples of Asia Minor

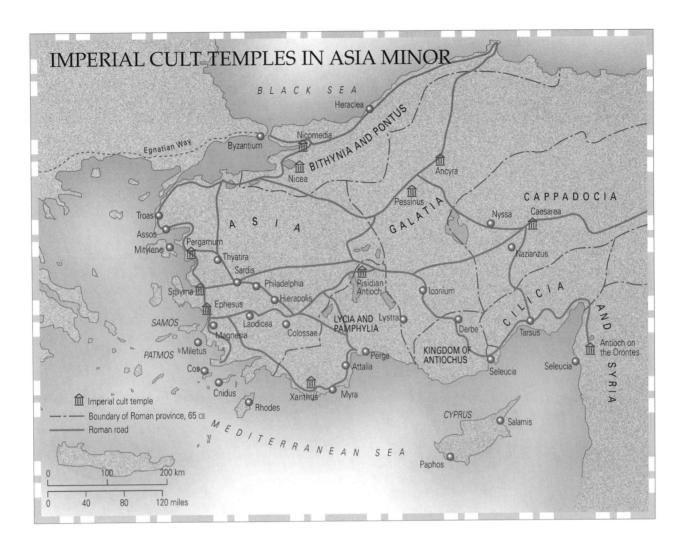

77. Map of the Myth of Nero Redivivus, or Nero Redux

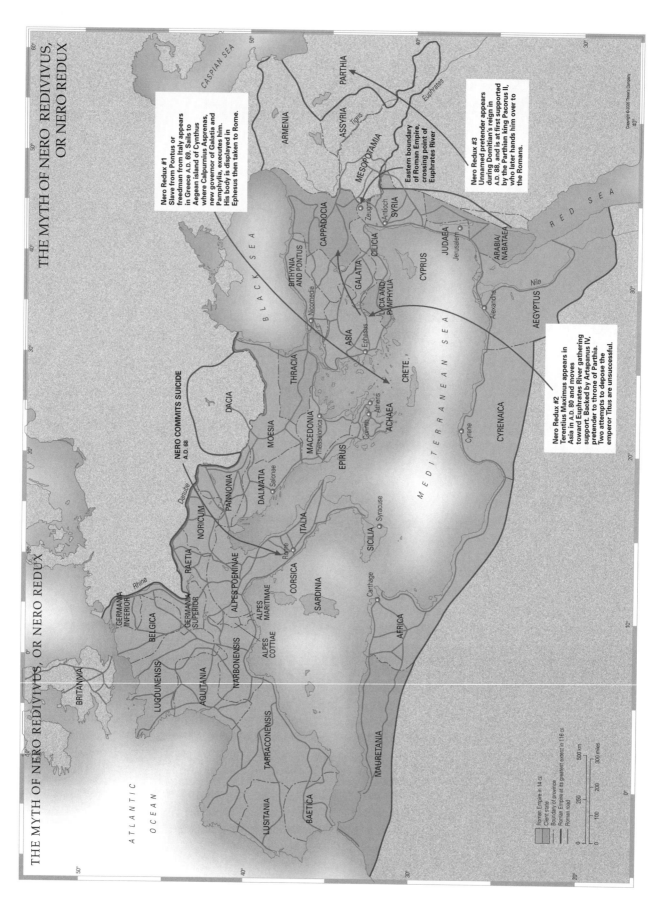

THE MYTH OF NERO REDIVIVUS, OR NERO REDUX

Nero Redux #1
Slave from Pontus or freedman from Italy appears in Greece A.D. 69. Sails to Aegean island of Cynthus where Calpurnius Asprenas, new governor of Galatia and Pamphylia, executes him. His body is displayed in, Ephesus then taken to Rome.

Nero Redux #3
Unnamed pretender appears during Domitian's reign in A.D. 88, and is at first supported by the Parthian king Pacorus II, who later hands him over to the Romans.

Eastern boundary of Roman Empire, crossing point of Euphrates River

Nero Redux #2
Terentius Maximus appears in Asia in A.D. 80 and moves toward Euphrates River gathering support. Backed by Artapanus IV, pretender to throne of Parthia. Two attempts to depose the emperor Titus are unsuccessful.

NERO COMMITS SUICIDE
A.D. 68

CASPIAN SEA

PARTHIA

ARMENIA

ASSYRIA

MESOPOTAMIA

Tigris

Euphrates

SYRIA

Antioch

Zeugma

JUDAEA

Jerusalem

ARABIA/ NABATAEA

RED SEA

CAPPADOCIA

BITHYNIA AND PONTUS

Nicomedia

GALATIA

CILICIA

CYPRUS

LYCIA AND PAMPHYLIA

ASIA

Ephesus

BLACK SEA

CRETE

AEGYPTUS

Alexandria

Nile

THRACIA

MACEDONIA

Thessalonica

EPIRUS

ACHAEA

Athens

Corinth

MEDITERRANEAN SEA

Cyrene

CYRENAICA

DACIA

MOESIA

DALMATIA

Salonae

PANNONIA

NORICUM

ITALIA

Rome

Syracuse

SICILIA

Carthage

AFRICA

RAETIA

ALPES POENINAE

ALPES MARITIMAE

ALPES COTTIAE

CORSICA

SARDINIA

GERMANIA INFERIOR

GERMANIA SUPERIOR

Rhine

Danube

BELGICA

LUGDUNENSIS

AQUITANIA

NARBONENSIS

BRITANNIA

TARRACONENSIS

LUSITANIA

BAETICA

MAURETANIA

ATLANTIC OCEAN

Roman Empire in 14 CE
Client state
Boundary of province
Roman Empire at its greatest extent in 116 CE
Roman road

0   100   250   500 km
0   100   200   300 miles

78. Map of Rome: City of Seven Hills

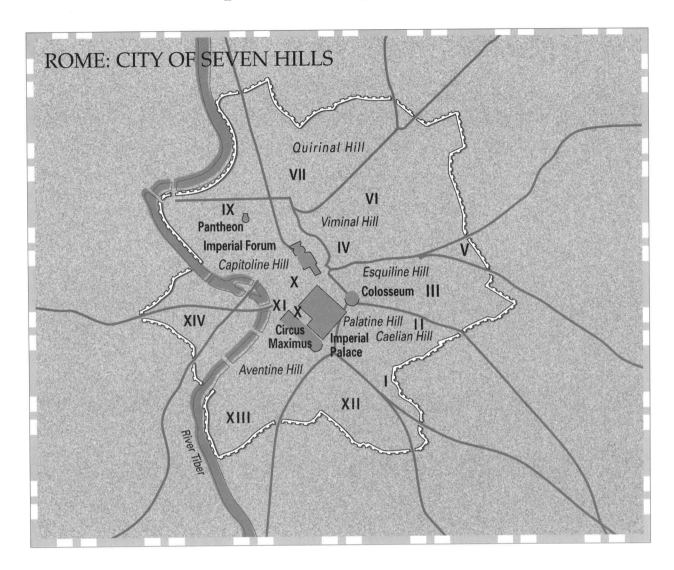

ROME: CITY OF SEVEN HILLS

Quirinal Hill

VII

VI

IX
Pantheon

Viminal Hill

Imperial Forum

IV

Capitoline Hill

X

Esquiline Hill

Colosseum   III

XI
X

Palatine Hill

II

XIV

Circus
Maximus

Imperial
Palace

Caelian Hill

I

Aventine Hill

XII

XIII

River Tiber

79. Map of Trade in the Roman Empire

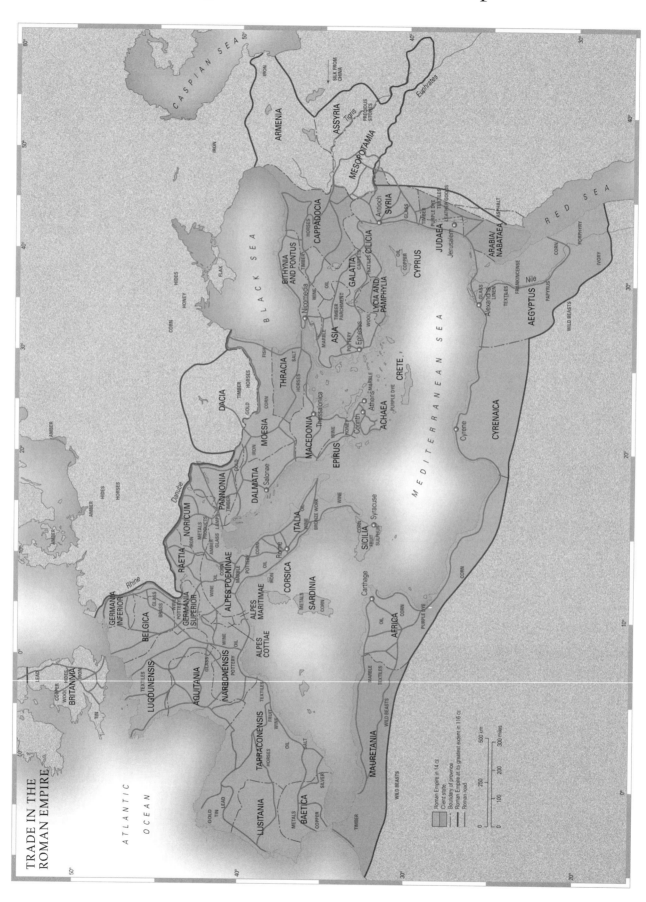

TRADE IN THE
ROMAN EMPIRE

Commentary and Sources Consulted

1. Authorship of Revelation

This chart is drawn primarily from my doctoral thesis, *A Pie in a Very Bleak Sky?* §1.2. The patristic evidence can be found in Justin (*Dial.* 81), Melito (see *Hist. eccl.* 4.26.2), Irenaeus (*Adv. Haer.* 3.11.1; 4.20.11; 4.35.2), Origen (*Matthew* 16.6), Tertullian (*Adv. Marc.* 3.14.3; 3.24.4), and Hippolytus (*De antichristo* 36–42). The testimony of Dionysius is found in Eusebius (*Hist. eccl.* 7.25.7–27). See also Donald Guthrie, *New Testament Introduction*, 932–48 and G. A. Williamson's incisive comment on the two Johns in *Eusebius: The History of the Church from Christ to Constantine*, 151n. 1.

2. Date of Revelation

This chart is drawn primarily from my article, "The Early Christians in Ephesus and the Date of Revelation, Again." See also Stephen Smalley, *Thunder and Love*, 40–48; David Aune, *Revelation*, 1:lvi–lxx; Gregory Beale, *Revelation*, 4–27.

3. Roman Empire in the Late First Century A.D.

The information used in this chart is drawn from a number of historical sources with Suetonius and Tacitus being the primary ones. Other excellent resources for the period are B. W. Henderson, *The Life and Principate of the Emperor Nero* and *Civil War and Rebellion in the Roman Empire, A.D. 69–70*; K. W. Wellesley, *The Long Year A.D.*; and B. W. Jones, *The Emperor Domitian*. I wish to thank S. R. F. Price for his suggestions as well as his review of the chart. Other charts of dates from the period can be found in *The Cambridge Ancient History*, 2nd ed., vols. 10 and 11, and at the beginning of Barbara Levick's *Vespasian*.

4. Time Line of the First-Century Church in Asia

Alternate chronologies for Paul can be found in W. M. Ramsay, *St. Paul Traveler and Roman Citizen*, 48; Robert Jewett, *Dating Paul's Life*, 95–104; and Loveday Alexander, "Chronology of Paul," in *Dictionary of Paul and His Letters*, 115–23. Paul Trebilco has developed a time line of the church in Ephesus in *The Early Christians in Ephesus from Paul to Ignatius*. The chronology of my chart differs, however, from some of Trebilco's conclusions on dating (and authorship). The historical situation drawn from the Pastoral Epistles largely follows the scenario developed by Gordon D. Fee, *1 and 2 Timothy, Titus*, 3–5.

5. Jewish and Christian Apocalypses

This chart was adapted from Mitchell Reddish, *Revelation*, 6. The information is also found in two articles in *Semeia*: "The Jewish Apocalypses" by John J. Collins, 21–59, and "The Early Christian Apocalypses" by Adela Yarbro Collins, 61–121. Note the two detailed charts on pages 28 and 104–5 respectively, which compare the different literary elements in all of these apocalypses. See also the numerous articles and books on apocalyptic literature that these two authors have written.

6. Literary Genres of Revelation

This chart was drawn from a number of sources, especially David Aune, *Revelation*, 1:lxx–xc; Grant Osborne, *Revelation*, 12–15; and F. D. Mazzaferri, *The Genre of the Book of Revelation from a Source-Critical Perspective*, 154, 181–84.

7. Chapter and Verse Counts with Text Set as Poetry

This chart, drawn from the UBS[4], the NIV, and the NKJV, demonstrates that poetry is also an important generic feature of Revelation. The NRSV follows the poetic formatting of UBS[4] except for one addition—Revelation 18:17. The NIV and the NKJV have only 404 verses because they include 12:18 with 13:1.

8. Words Occurring Only in Revelation (Hapax Legomena)

Revelation has a vocabulary of 916 words. The 108 words presented in this chart are never used elsewhere in the New Testament. (However, twenty proper nouns not occurring outside of Revelation are omitted.) The data in the chart is drawn from David Aune, *Revelation*, 1:ccvii–ccx, with corrections made to entries 1 and 85. Unlike Aune's chart, this chart is presented in textual order to assist the reader in translating these hapaxes. The English translations are drawn from the NRSV with several additions.

9. Allusions and Verbal Parallels in the Old Testament and Extrabiblical Literature

The references in this chart are drawn from the "Index of Allusions and Verbal Parallels" found in UBS[4], pages 891–901. The 403 verse citations with these allusions and verbal parallels are distributed as follows: Genesis—10; Exodus—24; Leviticus—4; Numbers—3; Deuteronomy—10 (Law—51); Judges—1; 1 Samuel—1; 2 Samuel—2; 1 Kings—6; 2 Kings—6; 1 Chronicles—1; 2 Chronicles—4; Nehemiah—1; Esther—1; Job—3; Psalms—69; Proverbs—3 (Writings—98); Isaiah—74; Jeremiah—37; Lamentations—1; Ezekiel—58; Daniel—41; Hosea—2; Joel—9; Amos—3; Obadiah—1; Micah—1; Nahum—1; Zephaniah—2; Zechariah—22; Malachi—2 (Prophets—254). The Law has 13 percent of the citations, the Writings 24 percent, and the Prophets 63 percent. UBS[4] does not list any quotations from the Old Testament in Revelation in its "Index of Quotations."

Discussion on the use of the Old Testament in Revelation can be found in all major commentaries on Revelation, with a recent comprehensive one in Gregory Beale, *Revelation*, 76–99. A monograph on the subject is Steve Moyise's *The Old Testament in the Book of Revelation*. See also Jon Paulien's useful evaluation, "Criteria and the Assessment of Allusions to the Old Testament in the Book of Revelation," in *Studies in the Book of Revelation*, edited by Steve Moyise, 113–29.

10. Structure of Revelation

J. Ramsey Michaels quips that "there are as many different outlines as there are interpreters" (*Interpreting the Book of Revelation*, 69). A look at the structural outlines in the many commentaries on Revelation quickly affirms Michaels's statement. Here are presented four different approaches to structure. The threefold structure based on 1:19 is espoused by many interpreters, including John Walvoord, *The Revelation of Jesus Christ*, 48. George Eldon Ladd (*A Commentary on the Revelation of John*, 14–17) bases his structural outline on the four "in the Spirit" experiences in Revelation. The chiastic structure is my own (*A Pie in a Very Bleak Sky?* §3.4.2.7), which builds on previous chiastic outlines proposed by E. W. Bullinger (*Commentary on Revelation*, 116), N. W. Lund (*Studies in the Book of Revelation*, 27, 34–35), E. Schüssler Fiorenza (*Revelation: Vision of a Just World*, 35–36), and K. A. Strand ("Chiastic Structure and Some Motifs in the Book of Revelation," 401). James L. Blevins (*Revelation as Drama*, 7–10) structures Revelation according to a drama with seven acts. Stephen S. Smalley (*The Revelation to John*, 21–22) likewise structures Revelation around seven scenes.

11. Identification of Christ with God in Revelation

This chart showing a chiastic pattern that identifies Christ with God is adapted from Richard Bauckham, *The Theology of the Book of Revelation*, 57.

12. Divine Names in Revelation

For a further discussion related to the theological importance of the divine names in Revelation, see Grant Osborne, *Revelation*, 31–47, and Richard Bauckham, *The Theology of the Book of Revelation*, passim.

13. Names for Believers in Revelation

Sophie Laws discusses the believers in Revelation in a stimulating essay called "The Lamb's Army" in *In the Light of the Lamb*, 52–68.

14. Apocalyptic Themes in Revelation, the Synoptic Gospels, and Pauline Epistles

The Synoptic tradition as found in the seven seals of Revelation 6 is found in chart 44. For the classic study on the synoptics, see Louis A. Vos, *The Synoptic Traditions in the Apocalypse*. See also D. Wenham, *The Rediscovery of Jesus' Eschatological Discourse*.

15. Thematic Parallels Between Revelation and John

The chart is loosely based on that by O. Böcher, "Apokalypse und Evangelium," in *L'Apocalypse johannique et l'Apocalyptique dans le Nouveau Testament*, 295–301; cf. J. du Rand, *Johannine Perspectives*, 245–46. For a discussion of eschatology in John's Gospel, see Stephen S. Smalley, *John: Evangelist and Interpreter*, 265–69.

16. Thematic Parallels Among Revelation, Jude, and 2 Peter

The chart is adapted from material found in J. A. T. Robinson, *Redating the New Testament*, 227.

17. Thematic Parallels Between Revelation and 4 Ezra

This chart is adapted from one in Wes Howard-Brook and Anthony Gwyther, *Unveiling Empire: Reading Revelation Then and Now*, 80. For other suggested parallels see G. H. Box, *The Ezra-Apocalypse*, 377. Fourth Ezra is also called 2 Esdras in the NRSV and the REB.

18. Theme of Victory in Revelation

This chart, utilizing the chiastic outline proposed earlier, shows how victory is, structurally, a macrodynamic theme for Revelation. The chart builds upon two charts found in Kenneth Strand, "'Overcomer': A Study of the Macrodynamic of Theme Development in the Book of Revelation," 239–240.

19. Theories of Interpretation of Revelation

See Grant Osborne, *Revelation*, 18–22, and Gregory Beale, *Revelation*, 44–49, for a further explication of these theories. The futurist view presented here is its most popular version, dispensational futurism. A modified futurism may hold that the church is the true Israel, that the Tribulation can be mid- or post-, that the visions may not be a sequence of future history arranged chronologically, and that the book may have symbolic elements.

20. Five Senses in Revelation

This chart focuses on John's visionary experience, which included all the senses. Stephen Smalley in *Thunder and Love* aptly writes regarding one of the senses: "The Apocalypse . . . seems to be full of colours. Prompted, no doubt, by his subject, John the Divine positively revels in colour, and paints his scenery vividly in a wide range of hues. . . . The set, against which the drama of Revelation is played out, is alive with evocative colour" (106–7).

21. Minerals, Gems, and Other Commodities in Revelation

The use of these images in Revelation is largely to connote the splendor and glory of the divine. Writing in reference to the gems specifically, Ben Witherington III in *Revelation*, 270, writes that the precious stones describe "how beautiful, precious, and holy the city is."

22. Symbols Interpreted in Revelation

An important first step for interpreting Revelation is to see how the book interprets itself. This chart presents all the symbols with their interpretations as found in Revelation. For a further discussion on symbolism and its interpretation in Revelation, see Gregory Beale, *Revelation*, 50–69.

23. Use of Numbers in Revelation

For a further discussion of the use of numbers in Revelation, see Gregory Beale, *Revelation*, 58–64, and Richard Bauckham, *Climax of Prophecy*, 29–37. See also Adela Yarbro Collins, *Cosmology and Eschatology in Jewish and Christian Apocalypticism*, 55–138.

24. Symbolism of Colors and Numbers in Revelation

This chart is adapted from two charts, one that is found in Jean-Pierre Prévost, *How to Read the Apocalypse*, 28–29, and the other in David Barr, *Tales of the End*, 8. See also I. T. Beckwith, *The Apocalypse of John*, 251–55; H. B. Swete, *The Apocalypse of St. John*, cccv–cccix; and Gregory Beale, *Revelation*, 58–64.

25. Figures of Speech in Revelation

Revelation is full of figurative language, so the examples given cannot be definitive. The meaning of each figure of speech is not given. For their interpretation consult any good commentary, such as David Aune's three-volume work. See also Gregory Beale's discussion of "A Method of Interpreting Symbols," in *Revelation*, 55–58.

26. Doublets in Revelation

The repeated use of doublets in Revelation is a structural phenomenon mentioned by most commentators. Some interpreters, e.g., Gregory Beale, *Revelation*, 530–32, also see two scrolls in Revelation: the scrolls with the seven seals (5:1) and the little scroll that John eats (10:2, 8–10). I interpret these two scrolls as one and the same.

27. Paired Characters in Revelation

This chart further develops the previous one and is based on several charts in James L. Resseguie, *Revelation Unsealed*, 124, 128, 142.

28. Angels and Demons in Revelation

For a brief discussion of the role of angels in Revelation, see Mark Wilson, *A Pie in a Very Bleak Sky?* §4.10.1. For specialized studies on the subject, see David Aune's Excursus 1C, "The 'Angels' of the Seven Churches," *Revelation*, 1:108–112, and L. T. Stuckenbruck's *Angel Veneration and Christology*.

29. Seven Beatitudes and Their Relationship to the Coming/Victor Sayings

Example 1 has the only two uses of ἀκούω ("I hear") and τηρέω ("I keep") together. Example 2 has the thematic relationship of death. Example 3 has the only two uses of κλέπτης ("thief") and the three uses of γρηγορέω ("I watch"). Example 4 has the only use of δειπνέω ("I eat") and its noun form δεῖπνον ("dinner"; apart from 19:17). Example 5 features the use of the distinctive phrase "second death" (also in 20:14; 21:8). Example 6, apart from the first beatitude, has the only other conjunction of λόγος ("word") and τηρέω ("I keep"). Example 7 features the use of the distinctive phrase "tree of life" (also in 22:2, 19). A connection also exists between beatitude 3 and the blame saying of the Laodicean letter (3:17, 18). Here are found the two references to believers as naked (γυμνός/γυμνότητός) with its resulting shame (αἰσχύνη/ἀσχημοσύνη). For a full discussion of the beatitudes in Revelation, see D. E. Hatfield's doctoral dissertation, "The Function of the Seven Beatitudes in Revelation."

30. Epithets of Jesus with Old and New Testament Background

See Gregory Beale's discussion of the verses in the chart elucidating the Old Testament background of the epithets, especially his "The Old Testament Background of Christ's Titles in 3:14," *Revelation*, 297–301.

31. Suggested Divisions of the Letters in Revelation 2–3

The chart represents divisions of the letters as suggested by five leading commentators: David Aune, *Revelation*, 1:184; E. Boring, *Revelation*, 86ff.; M. Hubert, "L'architecture des lettres aux Sept Églises (Apoc, ch II–III)," 349–50; J. H. Roberts, "A Letter to Seven Churches in the Roman Province of Asia," in *Reading Revelation*, 27; and F. Hahn, "Die Sendschreiben der Johannesapokalypse. Ein Beitrag zur Bestimmung prophetischer Redeformen," in *Tradition und Glaube*, 366–90. For more on the letter divisions, see Mark Wilson, *A Pie in a Very Bleak Sky?* §4.9.1. Hubert's French and Hahn's German titles are translated. Hubert's original titles are "L'adresse," "La titulature du Christ," "Le bilan positif," "Le bilan negative," "Les exhortations," "Les menaces," "La recompense"; Hahn's titles are "die Botenformel," "ὅιδα-Abschnitt," "der Weckruf," "der

"Überwinderspruch" (other German scholars use "Siegerspruch"—victor saying). Aune in an earlier volume, *Prophecy in Early Christianity and the Ancient Mediterranean World*, 275–79, suggested these divisions: (1) commissioning formula with Christological predications; (2) central "I know" section: (a) praise, (b) censure, (c) demand for repentance, (d) threat of judgment, (e) promise of salvation; (3) call for attention; (4) exhortation to conquer. Roberts sees threats to Philadelphia, Thyatira, and Laodicea; rewards for obedience to Thyatira, Sardis, Philadelphia, and Laodicea; encouragement to Sardis; and counsel to Laodicea.

32. Structure of the Seven Letters in Revelation 2–3

This chart is a synthesis of the preceding chart in addition to being drawn from the text of these seven prophetic letters. In the first three letters, the victor saying follows the hearing saying. Beginning with the letter to Sardis, the victor saying precedes the hearing saying. The reason for this structural change is unknown. For more on the literary structure of the seven letters, see Mark Wilson, *A Pie in a Very Bleak Sky?* §4.9.1; Gregory Beale, *Revelation*, 224–28; and David Aune, *Revelation*, 1:119–24.

33. An Imperial Edict Compared to the Letter to Ephesus

The edict on Jewish rights was issued by Augustus about 1 B.C. (Josephus, *Ant.* 16.162–165). The chart correlates portions of this Augustan edict with the letter to Ephesus based on the decretal analysis of M. Benner in *The Emperor Says: Studies in the Rhetorical Style in Edicts of the Early Empire*, 66–67, and David Aune, *Revelation*, 1:201–2. Aune (2:204) believes that "the seven proclamations of Rev. 2–3 are similar in form to ancient royal or imperial *edicts*." He never produces, however, a single edict that parallels the consistent form of the seven letters but instead gives parallels from sections of different edicts. In the chart above, while it is evident that some parallels do exist, significant differences can be found as well. Aune's conclusion, that the literary genre to which the seven letters belong is that of the imperial edict, remains unproven (2:183). For a fuller discussion of imperial edicts and Revelation, see Mark Wilson, *A Pie in a Very Bleak Sky?* §4.6.

34. Promise Images in the Seven Letters with Background in Jewish Literature

This chart is a synthesis of three charts found in Mark Wilson, *A Pie in a Very Bleak Sky?* §6.10.

35. Promises with Fulfillments and Relationship to Faithful Works

For the promises with fulfillments, see Mark Wilson, *A Pie in a Very Bleak Sky?* chapters 6–7 passim; for the relationship of faithful works to the promises, see R. C. Trench, *Commentary on the Epistles to the Seven Churches in Asia*, 97–98.

36. Rhetorical Situation of the Church in Revelation

For a further discussion, see Mark Wilson, *A Pie in a Very Bleak Sky?* §2.2. See also Elizabeth Schüssler Fiorenza's essay "Visionary Rhetoric and Social-Political Situation" in *The Book of Revelation: Justice and Judgment*, 181–203.

37. Wars and Battles in Revelation

War is a frequent theme in Revelation. A. Y. Collins in her *The Combat Myth in the Book of Revelation* has developed the thesis that the struggle in chapter 12 in particular is based on ancient Near Eastern combat myths. However, Gregory Beale (*Revelation*, 624–25) claims that, while John may be reflecting on such myths, he is interpreting them through the lens of Old Testament and Jewish traditions.

38. Theories of the Rapture from Revelation

This chart attempts to see what Revelation says concerning the rapture as interpreted from four perspectives. It purposely does not, however, draw from comparative texts in Daniel, the synoptics, or Paul. For a full discussion see Richard R. Reiter, Paul D. Feinberg, Gleason L. Archer, and Douglas J. Moo, *The Rapture: Pre-, Mid- or Post-Tribulational?* and Marvin Rosenthal, *The Pre-Wrath Rapture of the Church*, especially 231–41. As an alternative mid-tribulation view, Gleason Archer suggests that the rapture occurs in 14:14 (142–43).

39. Heavenly Throne-Room Vision with Parallels in Daniel

This chart is adapted from Gregory Beale, *Revelation*, 314–15.

40. Four Living Creatures with Background in Ezekiel and Isaiah

For further reading on the four living creatures, see R. H. Charles, *Revelation*, 1:119–24.

41. Identification of the Four Living Creatures with the Gospels

For the identification of the living creatures with the Gospels, see Grant Osborne, *Revelation*, 233n. 23.

42. Hymns of Revelation

Which units are to be identified as hymns is debated. Those selected reflect the consensus of most commentators. The arrows represent the continuation of an antiphonal unit. Carnegie points out rightly that, except for the hymn in 1:5b–6, all the other hymns occur within 4–19 (248) within five main sections (251), hence the breakdown in the chart. See David E. Aune, "Hymns in Revelation," in *Revelation*, 1:314–17, and David R. Carnegie, "Worthy Is the Lamb: The Hymns in Revelation," in *Christ the Lord*, 243–56. See also S. J. Friesen, *Imperial Cults and the Apocalypse of John*, 199.

43. Four Horsemen of the Apocalypse with Background in Zechariah

The four horsemen of the Apocalypse are one of the best known images from Revelation. Albrecht Dürer depicted them in a woodcut, and Ingmar Bergman featured them in his classic movie, *The Seventh Seal*. The colors of horse 3 in Zechariah 1:8 and horse 4 in Zechariah 6:3 vary among the translations. For the former, the NIV and NLT have "brown" while the NRSV and NKJV have "sorrel"; for the latter, the NIV and NKJV have "dappled" while the NRSV and NLT have "dappled gray." The Septuagint (LXX) reading in both verses is ψαροί. (See commentaries on Zechariah for the problems related to the Hebrew words for the colors.) For more on the Old Testament background of the horsemen, see Gregory Beale, *Revelation*, pp. 372–74. Beale emphasizes the punishment function of the horses in Zechariah. This motif is seemingly absent, however, in both pericopae. Instead, both visions refer to a "rest" on the earth that is discovered by the riders and chariots. The horsemen of Revelation do the opposite; they take rest from the world by inaugurating judgment.

44. Seven Seals and the Apocalypses in the Synoptic Gospels

Other identifications for the rider on the white horse have been suggested including Parthian invaders, Jesus Christ, and even the gospel itself. Compare the chart in R. H. Charles, *Revelation*, 1:158. See also L. Vos, *The Synoptic Traditions in the Apocalypse* for a complete study on the topic.

45. Possible Interrelationships Among the Seals, Trumpets, and Bowls

In the Simultaneous Perspective, the judgments are viewed as happening simultaneously. The repetition shows the intensification of the judgments. The Sequential Perspective sees the judgments individually and chronologically, holding to twenty-one in total. The Partial Recapitulation Perspective has features of the Simultaneous Perspective in that the seventh judgment in each cycle portrays the same wrath of God at the end. The judgments likewise show intensification with one-fourth, one-third, and finally 100 percent of the world being affected. In the Telescoping Perspective the seventh seal introduces and explains the seven trumpets and the seventh trumpet introduces and explains the seven seals. Thus the seventh seal is the seven trumpets, and the seventh trumpet is the seven bowls. Several of the charts are adapted from Robert G. Gromacki, *New Testament Survey*, 396–97; see also Gregory Beale, *Revelation*, 117–29.

46. Biblical Lists of the Twelve Tribes of Israel

Additional tribal lists with variations are found in Numbers 13:4–15; 34:19–28; and Ezekiel 48:31–34; only the lists in Numbers 34:19–28; Joshua 21:4–7; and 1 Chronicles 12:23–37 put Judah first among the tribes. There are also various listings of Jacob's twelve sons in the Old Testament—Genesis 35:23–26; Exodus 1:2–5; 6:14–25 (abbreviated); Numbers 26:5–62; 1 Chronicles 2:1–2; 2:3–7:40, in addition to the narrative of their births in Genesis 29–30. The omission of Simeon in Deuteronomy 33 is inexplicable, since that tribe was listed first in Deuteronomy 27:12 among those chosen to bless Israel on Mount Gerizim. See David Aune, *Revelation*, 2:460–65.

47. Trumpet and Bowl Judgments Compared to the Egyptian Plagues

Only six of the ten plagues appear in the trumpet and bowl judgments. Plagues 3 (gnats), 4 (flies), 5 (animal pestilence), and 10 (death of the firstborn) do not appear. See David Aune, *Revelation*, 2:498–506.

48. Vice Lists in Revelation Correlated to the Ten Commandments

The lists in 21:8 and 22:15 are compared for similarity, not order. See David Aune, *Revelation*, 2:545.

49. Identification of the Two Witnesses

In the messianic view, Joshua represents the Aaronic tradition of priest, while Zerubbabel represents the Davidic tradition of king. In the apocalyptic view the Antichrist will kill Enoch and Elijah at the end of the world, according to a tradition known to Augustine (*Ep.* 193.3, 5; *Gen. litt.* 9.5) and reflected also in the *Acts of Pilate* 25 found in the New Testament Apocrypha. The tradition also asserts that after three days, the two will be caught up in the clouds to meet the Lord. First Clement is an important early church document found in *The Apostolic Fathers*, dated by some scholars as early as A.D. 70. Another suggestion is that the two witnesses are the two Jewish high priests killed in A.D. 68. For more on the topic, see David Aune, *Revelation*, 2:598–603.

50. Time Periods of Persecution

For more on the subject of time and Revelation, see Mathias Rissi, *Time and History*. For more on the subject of persecution, see Adela Yarbro Collins, *Crisis and Catharsis*, 84–140, although I believe the situation faced by the Asian believers was real and not simply perceived.

51. Fall of Satan in Revelation

This chart is inspired by one in Gregory Beale, *Revelation*, 992, but goes in a very different direction. Beale argues that the parallels between chapters 12 and 20 suggest that these chapters depict the same events and mutually interpret one another. While they may mutually interpret one another, it is problematic to view them as depicting the same events. In fact, they depict a two-stage fall of Satan in Revelation, first from heaven to earth and then from earth to the Abyss. The first fall occurs at the Incarnation (cf. Luke 10:18), and the second at the Parousia.

52. Calculating the Number of the Beast (Gematria)

The Hebrew and Greek numbers used for calculating the number of the Beast, a process called gematria, are presented here. The Greek numerical system used several obsolete letters. For 6, a digamma was used. In medieval and modern usage, the numeral was normally written in the graphic form of ς, a final sigma. This form was historically distinct, however, from the digamma. The qoppa had the numerical value of 90, while the sampi had the numerical value of 900. The Greek form of Nero's name transliterated into Hebrew has a *nun* on the end. For more on the number of the Beast, see Richard Bauckham, *The Climax of Prophecy*, 384–407.

53. Two Marks of Revelation

Taw is the last letter of the Hebrew alphabet. During Ezekiel's day until the New Testament period the taw was written in the Old Hebrew script in the form of a cross (X). The Greek letter *chi*, the first letter of *Christos*, was recognized as an equivalent to taw. The Damascus Document (19.12) states that at the time of the Messiah's coming, quoting Ezekiel, that the only ones to be spared the sword are those marked by the taw.

Other references to the mark of the Beast include Revelation 14:9, 11; 16:2; 19:20; 20:4. Irenaeus's identification as Lateinos is found in *Against Heresies* 5.30.3. The gematria related to Jesus is found in *Sibylline Oracle* 1:324–30. The official titles of Domitian—ΑΥΤΟΚΡΑΤΩΡ ΚΑΙΣΑΡ ΔΟΜΕΤΙΑΝΟΣ ΣΕΒΑΣΤΟΣ ΓΕΡΜΑΝΙΚΟΣ (AUTOKRATOR KAISAR DOMETIANOS SEBASTOS GERMANIKOS)—were sometimes abbreviated on coins as in the chart; see Ethelbert Stauffer, "666," 237–44. For a full discussion of the topic, see David Aune, *Revelation*, 2:455–59, 766–73.

54. Thematic Parallels Between the Beast of Revelation and the Beasts of Daniel

See J. Fekkes, *Isaiah and Prophetic Traditions in the Book of Revelation*, 82–83; see also David Aune, *Revelation*, 3:941–44; and Gregory Beale, *Revelation*, 683–700. The letters of 1 and 2 John also refer to the Antichrist/Beast. The Antichrist denies that Jesus is the Christ (1 John 2:22), fails to confess that Jesus Christ has come from God (1 John 4:2–3), and deceives by saying that Jesus Christ has not come in the flesh (2 John 1:7). Also, the Antichrist has come and is coming (1 John 2:18; 4:3).

55. Portrait of the Beast in Revelation

This chart is adapted from David Aune, *Revelation,* 3:942–43.

56. Rise and Demise of the Evil Trinity

This chart again illustrates the use of chiasmus in Revelation's macrostructure and is adapted from K. A. Strand, "Chiastic Structure and Some Motifs in the Book of Revelation," 403.

57. Worship of the Emperor—the Beast of Revelation 13:4—Contrasted with Divine Worship

The specific nature of the worship of the Beast is not stated in Revelation. Roman writers, however, as well as inscriptions, mention various attributes that were used in honoring the emperor as a divine being. John's use of similar titles in Revelation is another example of irony in the book. Some of these inscriptions were found in the province of Asia. *IGR* 4.1756 was found at Sardis, and *OGIS* 458 was found in Apamea, with damaged copies being found at four other cities: Priene, Dorylaeum, Eumenea, and Maionia. *IGR* 4.331 from Pergamum calls Trajan the "Lord of the earth and the sea." For the role of worship in Asia's imperial cult, see S. R. F. Price, *Rituals and Power*, especially 188–206. Another use of "son of God" can be found in a letter from Augustus to Ephesus: "Emperor Caesar, son of the god Julius" (J. Reynolds, *Aphrodisias and Rome*, doc 12, line 1, p. 101).

58. Four *Hōde* (῟Ωδε "Here") Sayings of Revelation

For more on these sayings, see Mark Wilson, *A Pie in a Very Bleak Sky?* §4.12.1, and Wilson, "Revelation," *Zondervan Illustrated Bible Background Commentary*, 4:327.

59. Paired Angelic Revelations in Revelation

This chart is adapted from that of Charles Giblin, "Structural and Thematic Correlations in the Theology of Revelation 16–22," 487–504; see also David Aune, *Revelation*, 1:xcv–xcvii.

60. Historical Identification of the Seven Emperors (Rev. 17:9–11) in Relationship to the Twelve Caesars

Historic: This is the order in Suetonius, *The Twelve Caesars*; cf. Tacitus (*Ann.* 4.34; 13.3); Josephus (*Ant.* 18.32); Sibylline Oracles 5:12–51; and 4 Ezra 11–12. S. Giet, *L'Apocalypse et l'histoire*, 54, and J. M. Ford, *Revelation*, 290, follow 1–6 but opt for Vespasian as 7 and Titus as 8. J. B. Lightfoot, *The Apostolic Fathers*, 1.2.509, in interpreting the ten kings in *Epistle of Barnabas* 4:4, reckons the first king as Julius Caesar and the tenth as Vespasian.

Principate: Adopted by J. A. T. Robinson, *Redating the New Testament*, 243; A. A. Bell, "The Date of John's Apocalypse: The Evidence of Some Roman Historians Reconsidered," 93–102, and C. Rowland, *The Open Heaven*, 403–13.

Despotic: Adopted by H. B. Swete, *The Apocalypse of St. John*, 220, and R. H. Charles, *The Revelation of St. John*, 2:69. F. J. A. Hort, "The Apocalypse of St. John I–III," xxix, opts for Domitian as 7.

Roman Antichrist: Adopted by C. H. Turner, *Studies in Early Christian History*, 217, and E. B. Allo, *Saint Jean, l'Apocalypse*, 281–82.

Tyrannical: Adopted by E. Schüssler Fiorenza, *Revelation: Vision of a Just World*, 97, who falls one emperor short by failing to list Claudius.

Christological: Adopted by A. Strobel, "Abfassung und Geschichtstheolgie der Apokalypse nach Kp. 17, 9–12," 439–41. E. Schüssler Fiorenza, *The Book of Revelation: Justice and Judgment*, 42, states that this interpretation "finds its strongest support in Revelation . . . itself," yet changes the identification in her 1991 commentary.

For a Jewish apocalyptic perspective, see A. Yarbro Collins, *Crisis and Catharsis*, 64; for that of Christian persecution, see J. du Rand, *Johannine Perspectives*, 231.

Empires: Adopted by J. A. Seiss, *The Apocalypse*, 391–94, although the list of kingdoms is out of order. G. E. Ladd, *A Commentary on the Revelation of John*, 229, identifies only Rome as the sixth kingdom. W. Hendriksen, *More Than Conquerors*, 170–71, suggests a different first five: Old Babylonia, Assyria, New Babylonia, Medo-Persia, and Greco-Macedonia.

The symbolic approach to identifying the seven kings has been adopted by many interpreters (see David Aune, *Revelation*, 3:948 for a list). Richard Bauckham, *Climax of Prophecy*, 404–6, and Grant Osborne adopt a combination of the symbolical and historical views, that is, "the 5+1+1 does not refer to Roman emperors . . . but [is] a symbolic reference to the belief that the Roman tyranny was a temporary phenomenon about to be completed (in the seventh short-lived ruler) and would lead to the eschaton. Thus, the beast is the eighth emperor (17:11), who at the time of writing has not yet appeared. . . . This Antichrist is . . . one of the seven in the sense that he will follow their opposition to God and persecution of his people" (Osborne, *Revelation*, 620).

61. Trading Products of Revelation 18 in Relationship to Tyre and Rome

When the entire peninsula is included, the term Asia Minor is used. When a specific province of the empire is specified, that province will be used. For a general discussion of Asia Minor's trade products, see T. R. S. Broughton, "Roman Asia Minor," in *An Economic Survey of Ancient Rome*, 607–27. For the biblical background of John's list of trading products, see Richard Bauckham, *The Climax of Prophecy*, 350–67.

62. Last Battle in Revelation

This chart is based on the premise that there is one last battle depicted in Revelation. The three scenes show different perspectives and different participants, but the action is the same. For additional perspectives on this important topic, see the related discussions on these passages in various commentaries.

63. Messiah as an Eschatological Judge

This chart is adapted from material in J. Fekkes, *Isaiah and Prophetic Traditions in the Book of Revelation*, 118.

64. Interpretations of the 1,000 Years from Revelation 20:1–6

The name for the chart purposely does not use the word "millennium" because of its later theological connotations. It is imperative that the 1,000 years first be interpreted within its rhetorical function in Revelation itself. For further reading on the subject, see Darrell L. Bock, ed., *Three Views on the Millennium and Beyond*, and Robert G. Clouse, ed., *The Meaning of the Millennium: Four Views*. A number of charts representing these views can be found in Robert P. Lightner, *The Last Days Handbook*, 53–91.

65. Lists of Jewels in Antiquity

English versions usually translate "jacinth" for the eleventh jewel in Revelation (ὑάκινθος) as well as for the seventh jewel in Exodus and Ezekiel (λιγύριον; also in Josephus).

In the LXX list of Ezekiel 28:13, silver and gold are added after jasper. The different orders of jewels are presented with Josephus's alternate readings in parentheses. Only three of the twelve stones in Revelation differ totally in form from the lists in the LXX. G. B. Caird, *The Revelation of St. John the Divine*, 274–75, argues persuasively that John makes his own translation from the Hebrew for these stones. R. H. Charles, *The Revelation of St. John*, 2:167–68, argues, citing Kircher, that John's order is the exact reverse of the zodiac and hence a rejection of astrological speculations.

66. Paradise Motifs in Revelation and the Prophets

This chart has been created from material in the article "παράδεισος" by J. Jeremias, *Theological Dictionary of the New Testament*, 5:767n. 15. A chart with similar material appears in Jean-Pierre Prévost's *How to Read the Apocalypse*, 66. His entry titled "Universalism" has not been used because Revelation does not teach this concept. The "nations" (21:24) that inhabit the heavenly city are made up only of the victors from every nation "who have washed their robes and made them white in the blood of the Lamb" (7:9, 14).

67. Death and Resurrection in Revelation 19–22

This chart is inspired by the diagram in Gregory Beale's *John's Use of the Old Testament in Revelation*, 380; and idem, *Revelation*, 1005. I disagree with Beale that there is chiasm in the passage and instead see a linear progression as indicated by the arrows in the chart. Beale uses chiasm to interpret the first resurrection as spiritual. I am not persuaded that Alford's dictum is invalid: "If, in a passage where *two resurrections* are mentioned, . . . the first resurrection may be understood to mean *spiritual* rising with Christ, while the second means *literal* rising from the grave; then there is an end of all significance in language, and Scripture is wiped out as a definite testimony to any thing" (*Greek Testament*, 4.2:732). The burden of proof remains upon those who argue contrarily, and I have yet to see a convincing argument otherwise. The appearance of "first resurrection" in chapter 20, just before an implied "first" (first in fact, second in order) resurrection of the unrighteous suggests the identical sequence of two judgments in John 5:29. The spiritual resurrection of the saints living around the heavenly throne (e.g., 7:9; 14:1) has been depicted throughout the book, so there is no need to present a "spiritual" resurrection here in the narrative. The visions are all moving toward the end in the new heaven and new earth.

68. Architectural Features of the New Jerusalem

This chart is based on material from J. Fekkes, *Isaiah and Prophetic Traditions in the Book of Revelation*, 239.

69. Literary Parallels Between Revelation's Prologue and Epilogue

For more on these parallels, see David Aune, *Revelation*, 2:13–14; 3:1205–6.

70. Benedictions in the New Testament

See David Aune, *Revelation* 2:1240. His chart has been rearranged, a correction made in Romans 16:20, and his omission of Ephesians inserted.

71. Thematic Parallels Between Genesis 1–3 and Revelation

Many commentators have noted that Revelation's canonical place at the end of the New Testament and the Bible is particularly appropriate. It provides a fitting conclusion to the history of God's dealings with humanity begun in the book of Genesis. This chart is adapted from one found in *Halley's Bible Handbook*, 674.

72. Textual Evidence for Revelation

The chart is drawn from the following sources: Kurt Aland and Barbara Aland, *The Text of the New Testament*, 105ff., 155–59; David Aune, *Revelation*, 1:cxxxvi–clvi (however, there are six errors in the chart on p. cxxxix); Gregory Beale, *Revelation*, 70–75 (Beale does not include 𝔓[98]); Nestle-Aland, *Novum Testamentum Graece*, 27th ed.; and *The Greek New Testament*, 3rd and 4th eds. UBS[3] lists 13 Old Latin MSS; UBS[4] reduces the number to 6. It drops MSS c, dem, div, g[1], l, p; deletes MSS haf and m, and adds MS sin. Aune, *Revelation*, 1:clii–cliii presents the older list.

73. Canonical History of Revelation

The material for this chart was drawn from F. F. Bruce, *The Canon of Scripture*, passim, and Bruce M. Metzger, *The Canon of the New Testament*, passim.

74. Seven Churches Today

For more on the present state of the seven churches, see Mark Wilson, "Revelation," *Zondervan Illustrated Bible Background Commentary*, 4:376; Fatih Cimok, *A Guide to the Seven Churches*; and Clyde E. Fant and Mitchell G. Reddish, *A Guide to Biblical Sites in Greece and Turkey*.

75. Map of Roman Province of Asia

For this volume, Tim Dowley adapted his map of "The Church in Asia Minor" found in *The Kregel Bible Atlas*, 88. The seven churches lay along established Roman roads that a messenger would travel in delivering the document. The islands of Lesbos, Chios, Samos, Patmos, and Kos were part of the province of Asia in the first century. As the map shows, there were more than seven churches in Asia at the time of Revelation's writing. This is another indication of the symbolic usage of the number seven in the book. During the first century there were three imperial cult temples in Asia: at Pergamum built by Octavian (Augustus) in 29 B.C., at Smyrna built by Tiberius in A.D. 26, and at Ephesus built by Domitian in A.D. 89. For more on the Roman imperial cult, see S. R. F. Price, *Rituals and Power*.

76. Map of Imperial Cult Temples of Asia Minor

S. R. F. Price's volume *Rituals and Power* is the standard source on the topic. The maps found on pages xxii–xxv portray imperial cult activity for the first three centuries after Christ. While comprehensive regarding the subject, those maps prove anachronistic for the study of Revelation because the spread of the cult was more limited in the first century. Thus the number of temples depicted on the map here is more narrow. See also Stephen Mitchell, *Anatolia,* 1:100–117. I follow Mitchell in identifying the temples in Pessinus and Pisidian Antioch as imperial cult temples.

77. Map of the Myth of Nero Redivivus, or Nero Redux

Tacitus (*Hist.* 2.8.1) suggests that, in addition to the three documented on the map, there were at least two other pretenders. The elaboration of their activities, however, is lost. The ancient sources that discuss this myth are Tacitus, *Hist.* 2.8–9; John of Antioch, fr. 104; Suetonius, *Nero* 57; and Dio Chrysostom, *Or.* 21.10. See also Excursus 13A: "The Nero Redux or Redivivus Legend" in David Aune, *Revelation,* 2:737–39.

78. Map of Rome: City of Seven Hills

Rome was known throughout the ancient world as the city of seven hills. Numerous Roman writers (e.g., Juvenal, *Sat.* 9.130; Horace, *Carm. Saec.* 5; Ovid, *Trist.* 1.5.69; Pliny, *Nat.* 3.66–67) used the phrase "seven hills" as a locution for Rome. The names of the seven hills are inscribed on the base of a second-century A.D. statue found in Corinth. The statue apparently depicted Dea Roma sitting or standing on Rome's seven hills. For a brief discussion of these hills, see Mark Wilson, "Revelation," *Zondervan Illustrated Bible Background Commentary,* 4:346. The fire that is described as consuming "Babylon the Great" in Revelation 18:8–9, 18 had its antecedent in the fire of A.D. 64. Of Rome's fourteen districts, only four remained undamaged after the fire. Three were totally leveled, while the other seven displayed only the remains of half-burned relics of houses (*Ann.* 15.40). Nero blamed the Christians for this fire, and a great persecution broke out against the church. During this persecution both Peter and Paul were martyred publicly in Rome.

79. Map of Trade in the Roman Empire

Other maps portraying Roman trade can be found in Michael Grant, *Atlas of Ancient History,* 60–61; and A. A. M. van der Heyden and H. H. Scullard, *Atlas of the Classical World,* 127.

Bibliography

Aland, Kurt, and Barbara Aland. *The Text of the New Testament*. Grand Rapids: Eerdmans, 1987.

Alexander, Loveday. "Chronology of Paul." In *Dictionary of Paul and His Letters*, edited by Gerald F. Hawthorne et al. Downers Grove, IL: InterVarsity Press, 1993.

Alford, Henry. *The Greek Testament*. 4 vols. 1875. Reprint, Grand Rapids: Guardian, 1985.

Allo, E. B. *Saint Jean, l'Apocalypse*. 3rd ed. Paris: Gabalda, 1933.

Arnold, Clinton E., ed. *Zondervan Illustrated Bible Background Commentary*. 4 vols. Grand Rapids: Zondervan, 2002.

Aune, David E. *Prophecy in Early Christianity and the Ancient Mediterranean World*. Grand Rapids: Eerdmans, 1983.

———. *Revelation*. 3 vols. Word Biblical Commentary. Nashville: Thomas Nelson, 1997–1998.

Barr, David. *Tales of the End: A Narrative Commentary on the Book of Revelation*. Santa Rosa, CA: Polebridge, 1998.

Bauckham, Richard. *Climax of Prophecy*. Edinburgh: T & T Clark, 1999.

———. *The Theology of the Book of Revelation*. Cambridge: Cambridge University Press, 1993.

Beale, Gregory K. *The Book of Revelation*. New International Greek Testament Commentary. Grand Rapids: Eerdmans, 1999.

———. *John's Use of the Old Testament in Revelation*. Sheffield: Sheffield Academic Press, 1998.

Beckwith, I. T. *The Apocalypse of John*. New York: Macmillan, 1919.

Bell, A. A. "The Date of John's Apocalypse: The Evidence of Some Roman Historians Reconsidered." *New Testament Studies* 25 (1979): 93–102.

Benner M. *The Emperor Says: Studies in the Rhetorical Style in Edicts of the Early Empire*. Göteborg: Acts Universitatis Gothoburgensis, 1976.

Blevins, James L. *Revelation as Drama*. Nashville: Broadman & Holman, 1984.

Böcher, O. "Apokalypse und Evangelium." In *L'Apocalypse johannique et l'Apocalyptique dans le Nouveau Testament*, edited by J. Lambrecht. Gembloux: Ducolot/Leuven: Leuven University Press, 1980.

Bock, Darrell L., ed. *Three Views on the Millennium and Beyond*. Grand Rapids: Zondervan, 1999.

Boring, E. *Revelation*. Interpretation: A Bible Commentary for Teaching and Preaching. Louisville: John Knox, 1989.

Bowman, Alan K., Edward Champlin, and Andrew Lintott. *The Cambridge Ancient History: The Augustan Empire 43 B.C.–A.D. 69*. Vol. 10. 2nd ed. Cambridge: Cambridge University Press, 1996.

Bowman, Alan K., Peter Garnsey, and Dominic Rathbone. *The Cambridge Ancient History: The High Empire, A.D. 70–192*. Vol. 11. 2nd ed. Cambridge: Cambridge University Press, 2000.

Box, G. H. *The Ezra-Apocalypse*. London: Pitman, 1912.

Broughton, T. R. S. "Roman Asia Minor." In *An Economic Survey of Ancient Rome*. Vol. 4. Edited by Tenney Frank. Baltimore: Johns Hopkins, 1938.

Bruce, F. F. *The Canon of Scripture*. Downers Grove, IL: InterVarsity Press, 1988.

Bullinger, E. W. *Commentary on Revelation*. 1902. Reprint, Grand Rapids: Kregel, 1984.

———. *Figures of Speech Used in the Bible*. 1898. Reprint, Grand Rapids: Baker, 1968.

Caird, G. B. *The Revelation of St. John the Divine*. New York: Harper & Row, 1966.

The Cambridge Ancient History. 2nd ed. Vols. 10 and 11. Cambridge: Cambridge University Press, 2001, 2002.

Carnegie, David R. "Worthy Is the Lamb: The Hymns in Revelation." In *Christ the Lord: Studies Presented to Donald Guthrie*, edited by H. H. Rowdon. Downers Grove, IL: InterVarsity Press, 1982.

Charles, R. H. *The Revelation of St. John*. 2 vols. Edinburgh: T & T Clark, 1920.

Cimok, Fatih. *A Guide to the Seven Churches*. Istanbul: A Turizm Yayilari, 1998.

Clouse, Robert G., ed. *The Meaning of the Millennium: Four Views*. Downers Grove, IL: InterVarsity Press, 1977.

Collins, Adela Yarbro. *The Combat Myth in the Book of Revelation*. Missoula: Scholars Press, 1976.

———. *Cosmology and Eschatology in Jewish and Christian Apocalypticism*. Leiden: Brill, 1996.

———. *Crisis and Catharsis: The Power of the Apocalypse*. Philadelphia: Westminster, 1984.

———. "The Early Christian Apocalypses." *Semeia* 14 (1979): 61–121.

Collins, John J. "The Jewish Apocalypses." *Semeia* 14 (1979): 21–59.

Dowley, Tim. *The Kregel Bible Atlas*. Grand Rapids: Kregel, 2003.

du Rand, J. *Johannine Perspectives, Part 1: Introduction to the Johannine Writings*. Midrand, South Africa: Orion, 1991.

Fant, Clyde E., and Mitchell G. Reddish. *A Guide to Biblical Sites in Greece and Turkey*. Oxford: Oxford University Press, 2003.

Fee, Gordon D. *1 and 2 Timothy, Titus*. New International Biblical Commentary on the New Testament. Peabody, MA: Hendrickson, 1988.

Fekkes, J. *Isaiah and Prophetic Traditions in the Book of Revelation*. Sheffield: JSOT Press, 1994.

Ford, J. M. *Revelation*. Garden City, NY: Doubleday, 1975.

Friesen, S. J. *Imperial Cults and the Apocalypse of John*. Oxford: Oxford University Press, 2002.

Giblin, Charles. "Structural and Thematic Correlations in the Theology of Revelation 16–22." *Biblica* 55 (1974): 487–504.

Giet, S. *L'Apocalypse et l'histoire*. Paris: Presses Universitaires de France, 1957.

Grant, Michael. *Atlas of Ancient History*. London: Routledge, 1994.

Gromacki, Robert G. *New Testament Survey*. Grand Rapids: Baker, 1974.

Guthrie, Donald. *New Testament Introduction*. Downers Grove, IL: InterVarsity Press, 1990.

Hahn, F. "Die Sendschreiben der Johannesapokalypse. Ein Beitrag zur Bestimmung prophetischer Redeformen." In *Tradition und Glaube*, edited by G. Jeremias, G. H-W. Kuhn, H-W & H. Stegemann. Göttingen: Vandenhoeck & Ruprecht, 1972.

Halley, Henry H. *Halley's Bible Handbook*. Grand Rapids: Zondervan, 1962.

Hatfield, D. E. "The Function of the Seven Beatitudes in Revelation." Ph.D. diss. The Southern Baptist Theological Seminary, 1987.

Henderson, B. W. *Civil War and Rebellion in the Roman Empire, A.D. 69–70*. London: Macmillan, 1908.

———. *The Life and Principate of the Emperor Nero*. London: Macmillan, 1903.

Hendriksen, William. *More Than Conquerors: An Interpretation of the Book of Revelation*. Grand Rapids: Baker, 1940.

Hort, F. J. A. "The Apocalypse of St. John I–III." In *Expository and Exegetical Studies*. 1908. Reprint, Minneapolis: Klock & Klock, 1980.

Howard-Brook, Wes, and Anthony Gwyther. *Unveiling Empire: Reading Revelation Then and Now*. Maryknoll, NY: Orbis, 1999.

Hubert, M. "L'architecture des lettres aux Sept Églises (Apoc, ch II–III)." *Revue Biblique* 3 (1960): 349–53.

Jewett, Robert. *Dating Paul's Life*. London: SCM, 1979.

Jones, B. W. *The Emperor Domitian*. London: Routledge, 1992.

Kittel, G., and G. Friedrich, eds. *Theological Dictionary of the New Testament*. 10 vols. Grand Rapids: Eerdmans, 1964–1976.

Ladd, George Eldon. *A Commentary on the Revelation of John*. Grand Rapids: Eerdmans, 1972.

Laws, Sophie. *In the Light of the Lamb: Imagery, Parody, and Theology in the Apocalypse of John*. Wilmington: Michael Glazier, 1988.

Levick, Barbara. *Vespasian*. New York: Routledge, 1999.

Lightfoot, J. B. *The Apostolic Fathers*. 1889–90. 5 vols. Reprint, Grand Rapids: Baker, 1981.

Lightner, Robert P. *The Last Days Handbook*. Nashville: Thomas Nelson, 1990.

Lund, N. W. *Studies in the Book of Revelation*. Chicago: Covenant Press, 1955.

Mazzaferri, F. D. *The Genre of the Book of Revelation from a Source-Critical Perspective*. New York: de Gruyter, 1989.

Metzger, Bruce M. *The Canon of the New Testament: Its Origin, Development, and Significance.* Oxford: Clarendon, 1987.

Michaels, J. Ramsey. *Interpreting the Book of Revelation.* Grand Rapids: Baker, 1992.

Mitchell, Stephen. *Anatolia.* 2 vols. Oxford: Clarendon, 1993.

Moyise, Steve. *The Old Testament in the Book of Revelation.* Sheffield: Sheffield Academic Press, 1995.

Osborne, Grant R. *Revelation.* Baker Exegetical Commentary on the New Testament. Grand Rapids: Baker, 2002.

Paulien, Jon. "Criteria and the Assessment of Allusions to the Old Testament in the Book of Revelation." In *Studies in the Book of Revelation*, edited by Steve Moyise. Edinburgh: T & T Clark, 2001.

Prévost, Jean-Pierre. *How to Read the Apocalypse.* New York: Crossroad, 1993.

Price, S. R. F. *Rituals and Power: The Roman Imperial Cult in Asia Minor.* Cambridge: Cambridge University Press, 1984.

Ramsay, W. M. *St. Paul the Traveler and Roman Citizen.* Revised by Mark Wilson. Grand Rapids: Kregel, 2001.

Reddish, Mitchell. *Revelation.* Macon: Smyth & Helwys, 2001.

Reiter, Richard R., Paul D. Feinberg, Gleason L. Archer, and Douglas J. Moo. *The Rapture: Pre-, Mid- or Post-Tribulational?* Grand Rapids: Zondervan, 1984.

Resseguie, James L. *Revelation Unsealed: A Narrative Critical Approach to John's Apocalypse.* Leiden: Brill, 1998.

Reynolds, Joyce. *Aphrodisias and Rome.* London: Society for the Promotion of Roman Studies, 1982.

Rissi, Mathias. *Time and History.* Richmond: John Knox, 1966.

Roberts, J. H. "A Letter to Seven Churches in the Roman Province of Asia." In *Reading Revelation*, edited by J. E. Botha, P. G. R. de Villiers, and J. Engelbrecht. Pretoria: van Schaik, 1988.

Robinson, J. A. T. *Redating the New Testament.* London: SCM, 1976.

Rosenthal, Marvin. *The Pre-Wrath Rapture of the Church.* Nashville: Nelson, 1990.

Rowland, C. *The Open Heaven.* New York: Crossroad, 1982.

Schüssler Fiorenza, Elizabeth. *The Book of Revelation: Justice and Judgment.* Philadelphia: Fortress, 1985.

———. *Revelation: Vision of a Just World.* Philadelphia: Fortress, 1991.

———. "Visionary Rhetoric and Social-Political Situation." In *The Book of Revelation: Justice and Judgment*, 181–203. Philadelphia: Fortress, 1985.

Scullard, H. H. *Atlas of the Classical World.* London: Thomas Nelson, 1959.

Seiss, J. A. *The Apocalypse: Lectures on the Book of Revelation.* 1900. Reprint, Grand Rapids: Zondervan, 1975.

Smalley, Stephen S. *John: Evangelist and Interpreter.* Downers Grove, IL: InterVarsity Press, 1998.

———. *The Revelation to John.* Downers Grove, IL: InterVarsity Press, 2005.

———. *Thunder and Love: John's Revelation and John's Community.* Milton Keynes, U.K.: Word, 1994.

Stauffer, Ethelbert. "666." *Coniectanea Neotestamentica* (1947): 237–44.

Strand, Kenneth A. "Chiastic Structure and Some Motifs in the Book of Revelation." *Andrews University Seminary Studies* 16.2 (1978): 401–8.

———. "'Overcomer': A Study of the Macrodynamic of Theme Development in the Book of Revelation." *Andrews University Seminary Studies* 28 (1990): 239–40.

Strobel, A. "Abfassung und Geschichtstheolgie der Apokalypse nach Kp. 17, 9–12." *New Testament Studies* 10 (1963–1964): 439–41.

Stuckenbruck, L. T. *Angel Veneration and Christology: A Study in Early Judaism and in the Christology of the Apocalypse of John.* Tübingen: J. C. B. Mohr (Paul Siebeck), 1995.

Swete, H. B. *The Apocalypse of St John.* 3rd ed. London: Macmillan, 1909.

Trebilco, Paul. *The Early Christians in Ephesus from Paul to Ignatius.* Tübingen: J. C. B. Mohr (Paul Siebeck), 2004.

Trench, R. C. *Commentary on the Epistles to the Seven Churches in Asia.* London: Macmillan, 1883.

Turner, C. H. *Studies in Early Christian History.* Oxford: Clarendon, 1912.

van der Heyden, A. A. M., and H. H. Scullard. *Atlas of the Classical World.* London: Thomas Nelson, 1959.

Vos, Louis A. *The Synoptic Traditions in the Apocalypse.* Kampen: J. N. Kok, 1965.

Walvoord, John F. *The Revelation of Jesus Christ.* Chicago: Moody, 1966.

133

Wellesley, K. W. *The Long Year A.D. 69*. 2nd ed. Bristol: Bristol Classical Press, 1989.

Wenham, David. *The Rediscovery of Jesus' Eschatological Discourse*. Sheffield: JSOT Press, 1984.

Williamson, G. A. *Eusebius: The History of the Church from Christ to Constantine*. Harmondsworth, U.K.: Penguin, 1965.

Wilson, Mark. "The Early Christians in Ephesus and the Date of Revelation, Again," *Neotestamentica* 39.1 (2005): 163–93.

———. *A Pie in a Very Bleak Sky? Analysis and Appropriation of the Promise Sayings in the Seven Letters to the Churches in Revelation 2–3*. Pretoria: University of South Africa, 1996.

———. "Revelation." In *Zondervan Illustrated Bible Background Commentary*, edited by Clinton E. Arnold, 4:244–383. Grand Rapids: Zondervan, 2002.

Witherington, Ben III. *Revelation*. New Cambridge Bible Commentary. Cambridge: Cambridge University Press, 2003.

See and Hear Flashcards on Your MP3 Player, Cell Phone, and Computer!

The iVocab package helps students learn vocabulary by combining flashcards with audio reinforcement. Using the premade slideshows included in iVocab, students are now able to see and hear vocabulary followed by the translation. Chapter vocabulary from a number of widely used grammars is included. These audio-video flashcards can be used on the Apple iPod mobile digital device (both video and photo models), video cell phones, and computers (PC and Mac). Students with other MP3 players can still access and utilize the audio presentations.

iVocab Biblical Greek   *Available August 2007*
David M. Hoffeditz and J. Michael Thigpen
DVD-ROM | ISBN 978-0-8254-2756-5 | 926 flashcards

iVocab Biblical Hebrew   *Available August 2007*
David M. Hoffeditz and J. Michael Thigpen
DVD-ROM | ISBN 978-0-8254-2755-8 | 2,187 flashcards

Kregel
Academic & Professional

New in New Testament Studies

Four Views on the Warning Passages in Hebrews
Herbert W. Bateman IV, general editor
This definitive resource explores the original and contemporary meaning of the oft-neglected, difficult "warning passages." Contributors include Gareth L. Cockerill, Buist M. Fanning, Grant R. Osborne, Randall C. Gleason, and George H. Guthrie.
464 pp. • pb • ISBN 978-0-8254-2132-7

Faithful Feelings
Rethinking Emotion in the New Testament
Matthew A. Elliott
I. Howard Marshall: "There is no other book that covers the same ground, and the topic is an important one."
304 pp. • pb • ISBN 978-0-8254-2542-4

Two Gospels from One
A Comprehensive Text-Critical Analysis of the Synoptic Gospels
Matthew C. Williams
Scot McKnight: "[Proposes] a method—textual criticism—that has within it the secret to resolving the Synoptic Problem on as objective grounds as we are likely to find. . . . A severe challenge for alternative theories."
256 pp. • pb • ISBN 978-0-8254-3940-7

Kregel
Academic & Professional